PICTORIAL SOUVENIRS
OF BRITAIN

PICTORIAL SOUVENIRS
OF BRITAIN

IAN T. HENDERSON

DAVID & CHARLES
NEWTON ABBOT LONDON
NORTH POMFRET (VT) VANCOUVER

ISBN 0 7153 6660 2

Library of Congress Catalog Card Number
74-83321

Set in 11 on 12pt Plantin and printed in
Great Britain by Biddles Limited Guildford
for David & Charles (Holdings) Limited
South Devon House Newton Abbot Devon

Published in the United States of America
by David & Charles Inc North Pomfret
Vermont 05053 USA

Published in Canada by Douglas David &
Charles Limited 3645 McKechnie Drive
West Vancouver BC

Contents

Introduction

This book is not about antiques which tend to be expensive, but rather about bygones, curios and bric-a-brac which should be less expensive, and it is also about lots of other things which can develop from small beginnings. It all started from pictures and the few odd pieces of china picked up because each had a view of a familiar place, but although the place was familiar the scene had changed and the horses had gone, the sailing ships had gone and the people had altered their mode of dressing. One wet Saturday in March 1966, instead of going to the local Point to Point, my wife and I browsed through the St Mary's Road district of Southampton where there were a number of bric-a-brac and junk shops, but with no particular intention of buying anything. We came back with six little china pieces—a cruet, a bell, a beaker and three vases featuring Weymouth (2), Bournemouth, Brighton, Salisbury and Land's End. The total bill was 97½p (19/6d). For the first time we saw the expression 'A Present from . . .' and there were china marks on three of them together with a printed 'Made in Germany' on some, and 'Austria' on another. From this humble beginning we launched into the world of collecting pictorial souvenirs, and all the fun of enquiring how everything started and who made what and when.

Today, with the active help of my wife, we have built up a collection of some 900 pieces which have cost less than a thousand pounds. We have learnt something about the heyday of these souvenirs from 1880–1914, something about the large Continental imports during this time, and a little about how the British produced their own souvenirs from those early 'Trifles from . . .' at the end of the eighteenth century until more modern times. It would be difficult to find a field which provokes more enquiry about pottery and porcelain and manufacturers long since defunct, and for going off and comparing the views of not so long ago with those of today and maybe photographing them. What it has revealed is a vast field for collecting and enquiry for those who want to start, and are prepared to begin with what appears to be bric-a-brac requiring modest expense. This book is, therefore, primarily for the new collector but also for those collectors who already take an interest in this subject and would like to know more about it. By including something of the historical background of the places that have achieved souvenir status, we hope that it is also a book for those who enjoy reading about yesterday with no thought of collecting.

Acknowledgements

I first met A. W. Coysh as the author of two books on Staffordshire Blue and was fortunate to arouse his interest and that of his photographer, Richard Clements, in pictorial souvenirs. Bill Coysh has researched many of the subject matters of the souvenirs, and in doing so widened the interest of the book, besides helping with the task of selecting and annotating all the items illustrated. Richard Clements has taken the photographs; Caroline Leete and Janet Robertson have prepared the final manuscript. My thanks are, therefore, due to an experienced team, all of whom made the production of the book an enjoyable experience.

My thanks are also due to Mr J. P. Cushion of the Victoria & Albert Museum, for his help on the continental manufacturers and their marks. I am grateful also to Mrs P. Asa Thomas, Mr David Martineau and Mr A. E. Burnett for their help.

1 Pictorial Souvenirs

The technical description of what we propose to write about is topographical china, wood, glass, metal, or indeed any other substance—with the exception of paper—on which a named picture of a locality can be placed. Apart from the plurality of names required (they hardly slip off the tongue with conviction) and in the absence of a generally accepted term, we propose to use 'Pictorial Souvenirs' to cover all articles, whatever they are made of, provided they were intended to be souvenirs and carry a named view of a place. At the present time the expression 'View China' is often heard and is descriptive enough as far as it goes, but excludes other materials and, in the absence of an accepted term, it is difficult to explain to any dealer what you are looking for.

There are any number of ornaments and other articles which have the caption 'A present from . . .', but they do not carry any illustrations, and it is those which do carry one that provide the whole reason for writing this book. If the view is named, there was no particular point in adding the caption 'A Present from . . .' because it was a glimpse of the obvious and could hardly have come from anywhere else; nevertheless, quite a number of these pictorial souvenirs do carry this caption and they happen to be those which have been manufactured on the Continent. The ornaments themselves can provide worthwhile study but it is the pictures which are so fascinating and so worth looking at and comparing with the same scene today. We know of no other form of collecting which provides two collector's items for the price of one.

The building up of a collection of pictorial souvenirs involves searching for anything which has a picture on it because, as yet, few understand what you are really looking for and in any case the looking is fun. The china is easy enough to recognise and may be found in antique centres and Hypermarkets or anywhere where Victoriana and bric-a-brac are sold, but there are all sorts of other unexpected souvenir items which may turn up. The ivory paper knife (Plate No. 1) is an example.

1 Ivory paper knife with a tiny glass insert in the handle (less than 0·1″
diam.) which when held to the light shows six views called 'Memories
of the Isle of Wight'.
Length 8″ (20·3 cm.)

When starting, there is a tendency to buy everything that is available, but later one establishes a criterion. Firstly, is the piece interesting in itself, i.e. a shaving mug or moustache cup; or, secondly, is the picture? Quite often they both are, and that is fine, but if, for instance, you are offered a plate with a view of the Town Hall of some town you have no particular wish ever to visit, there may be no point in acquiring it. The quality and interest of the picture has, to us, always been important, particularly where the contrast with the scene today is most vivid. Further occupation is also provided by taking souvenirs and visiting their birthplaces and trying to photograph the souvenir scenes as they are today; they show up even better on slides, especially if the original souvenir and its view can also be shown. We have confined our collections entirely to British scenes, but there are plenty of souvenirs around with Continental views and to anyone who likes touring with an objective, they might make another collector's field.

We shall be discussing the history of pictorial souvenirs as far as present knowledge will take us, but the collecting of early pieces goes beyond the price bracket intended for this book. The main part of our collection is dated between 1880–1914; they are not artistic masterpieces but many are attractive ornaments. They belong to a period less than a hundred years ago and are not yet technically antiques, but they record modestly the last of an era which ended with the First World War and to the present generation they are antique. In looking at the history we have been anxious to find out who manufactured the British and the Continental souvenirs. There are a great many unmarked pieces and we have always been on the lookout for china marks. We recommend the most careful examination of new acquisitions because some impressed marks are most difficult to spot. It is the existence of these marks which adds another source of enquiry to this field and has in itself taught us a great deal about British china and enabled us to identify a number of the German and Austrian manufacturers who exported to this country during this period. These souvenirs, both English and foreign, were originally extremely cheap and the information regarding the trade at this time is sparse, with few books of reference to help us. By publishing this book we hope that others may be able to add to this general survey of a wide field by concentrating their collecting more on the works of individual manufacturers both British and foreign, or on articles within the whole range of souvenirs such as ribbon plates, teapots, paperweights, etc., and in doing so find the answers to many intriguing questions. We do not know, for instance, how the German and Austrian exporters handled their distribution in this country nor how they obtained their pictures of British scenes, and yet this business was carried on almost within living memory.

There are, however, several subjects related to pictorial souvenirs on which books have been written and which are also concerned with named views of places.

The first of these is 'Commemorata', which differ only from souvenirs in that they are intended to commemorate an event such as a coronation or a person who was distinguished in some way, and these include the well known Staffordshire figures. There are quite a number of cases where commemorata contain interesting views and are of equal interest to collectors of pictorial souvenirs. A recently published book on the subject is *Commemorative Pottery* by J. and J. May, published in 1972.

Pot lids are the second related subject. These were attractively decorated pots containing anything from bear's grease to meat or fish paste. The lids with named views of places are undoubtedly interesting but can hardly be called pictorial souvenirs in our sense of the term. The only pot lids we have in our collection are in a series showing a dozen of the Cambridge Colleges, Harrow School and Windsor (Plate No. 97b); they can be dated to the early part of this century but we have not yet been able to establish what their pots contained. Finally, there are Stevengraphs, which are machine-made silk pictures on a variety of subjects and include a number of named views of places. They were invented by Thomas Stevens of Coventry and first sold at the

York Exhibition of 1879. See Geoffrey Godden's book *Stevengraphs and other Victorian Silk Pictures* (1971).

These three subjects, Commemorata, Pot Lids and Stevengraphs have all been thoroughly researched and written about and, although the original cost was extremely small, they have become popular collector's items and achieved prices in the leading Auction Rooms which would have been undreamed of not long ago. This must be a source of satisfaction to those early collectors who bought prior to the popularity subsequently acquired, but it makes them expensive for the newcomer.

There is one book which does deal admirably with one section of Pictorial Souvenirs and that is *Tunbridge and Scottish Souvenir Woodware* by Edward H. and Eva R. Pinto (1970) which is referred to again later. In spite of this book, which gives all the information on the subject which could be desired, these souvenirs still remain at reasonable prices. We have a small collection (see examples, Plate No. 2) which perhaps is more interesting for the variety of the range than for the views, which are small and not as clear as they might be if placed on china.

2 Pinholder, 'housewife', snuff box and two match holders with printed views respectively of Tighnabruaich (the first two), Ben Nevis, Stirling Castle and Norham Castle.

We have been asked whether in writing a book about pictorial souvenirs it will perform the same function for them and prices will rise in a similar way. Prices depend on supply and demand and the supply should be substantial with thousands of pieces in homes all over the country, some held with sentimental regard but others regarded as rubbish and often disposed of as 'junk'. A realisation that they may have a modest value could improve the market supply, and encourage dealers to become more familiar with the subject. At the moment, few hold anything but a modest stock and it is for this reason that it is not possible to quote prices. To do so might only lead to disappointment. As is explained later, English pieces tend to be of better quality than the foreign and are priced accordingly, especially those made by leading British manufacturers. There will also always be a premium if a piece is sold in its own locality and, regardless of the picture, objects such as moustache cups and shaving mugs are already in some demand, as are cottages. With the leading Auction Rooms now dealing in Victoriana and the later periods, souvenirs are already appearing in the catalogues including such items as Goss Armorial China. It looks therefore as though there may be improved marketability through this source as well. We can at least say that the market for pictorial souvenirs should be wide enough to cater for all pockets; there will be expensive and fashionable items but you do not have to buy them, and there will be less costly alternatives.

All books on antiques advise collectors to buy undamaged pieces and this must be sound advice, but in our case the question of whether or not to buy a damaged piece has depended on the picture and the same thing has gone for the cup without the saucer and vice versa. If the view is unusual and of good quality you may not get another opportunity to do better.

It may sound obvious, but it is worthwhile to catalogue everything as soon as you buy it. Record a description of each piece, numbering and labelling it, give the date purchased, the cost and from whom acquired and, finally, the place with notes such as manufacturer's mark or country of origin. A separate index of place names is also required. The reference books that you will find handy are:

The Handbook of British Pottery & Porcelain Marks by G. A. Godden

Pocket Book of German Ceramic Marks and those of other Central European Countries by J. P. Cushion.

Other books may be obtained through your local Reference Library. Librarians are always most helpful in obtaining books which are not held locally.

We have tried to keep the use of technical terms to a minimum, but some must be used and these are explained in the glossary on page 158.

There are also opportunities for joining a Collectors' Club. Most of these are linked in with two national organisations. If you write to the Secretaries they will inform you if there is a club in your area. They are:

The Antique Collectors' Club, Clopton, Woodbridge, Suffolk

and the

Decorative and Fine Arts Societies, Woodland, Looseley Row, Aylesbury, Bucks.

2 The Souvenir Instinct

Today the souvenir and gift trades flourish all over the world as never before and at home every conceivable anniversary is being commemorated in no ordinary way. This can only be explained as being the exploitation for good business reasons of the instinct in people to collect for themselves a piece of something memorable, given the opportunity. This instinct in its worst form is recognised by the term 'souvenir hunters' who, given half a chance, will strip a crashed aeroplane and who used to reduce the initialled cutlery of the old pre-nationalised railway companies by a steady annual toll. The souvenir in its best sense can also be used as a gift and presupposes a journey or travel and the wish to remember friends and relatives by giving them a present on returning, although today this can be done at small cost by means of a postcard to a wide circle of friends. We are interested in knowing when commercial souvenirs were first recorded because we learn that from Biblical times those who went on journeys both gave and received gifts from those that they visited. What did the Crusader, for instance, send or bring back from the Holy Land in the twelfth century, or the pilgrims from Canterbury? We have to start much later with the evidence given in the Pinto's book on *Tunbridge & Scottish Woodware* about the rise and decline of souvenirs in wood. In so doing they have established for Tunbridge Ware a claim to be a pioneer of souvenirs. This woodware was to enjoy a long period of prosperity, the craft was traditional and provided a wide range of useful presents which nevertheless were not cheap. They were to remain supreme whilst wood had no competitive material and their decline in popularity started with the development of pottery and porcelain souvenirs. A quotation they give from the *History of Tunbridge Wells* by Benge Burr, 1766, is worth quoting: 'The trade of Tunbridge Wells is similar to that of Spa in Germany and chiefly consists of a variety of toys in wood, such as tea chests, dressing boxes, snuff boxes, punch ladles, and numerous other little articles of the same kind. Of these, great quantities are sold to the company in summer, especially at their leaving the place, when it is customary for them to take Tunbridge fairings to their friends at home.' Earlier quotations make it apparent that the trade had already been established for nearly a century but it is to be noted that the word 'fairings' is applied to a Spa at this time. We also note that the instinct to support a market in souvenirs and gifts was already there, and was being stimulated by the growth in the number of spas and by the desire to travel and discover Britain.

THE PICTURES

It must be appreciated that in the middle of the eighteenth century few people had any idea of what the rest of the country looked like. The general populace did not travel, communications were poor and only the wealthy had any idea what London and the other cities looked like because they had been there. The illustration of places or landscapes, as they are known, is surprisingly recent; the painters of the sixteenth and seventeenth centuries painted portraits and religious subjects. The landscape first appeared as a background to a portrait and only gradually moved into the foreground with figures appearing as part of the landscape. At this stage people began to see what the countryside really looked like. We then had the English watercolour school in the middle of the eighteenth century. *The Discovery of Britain* (1964) by Esther Moir tells how modern tourism started, how visits to all the big houses took place and describes the study of the 'picturesque' in Wales, Scotland, Ireland and the Lake District. In a surprisingly short space of time, artists started publishing prints illustrating the beauties of the countryside and the big houses with descriptions of their grandeur. They were sold to a limited public eager to learn what other people's houses looked like and able to consider whether they themselves should organise a tour and discover the country they lived in. These are the source prints from which so many of the early landscapes painted on English porcelain were taken, although the articles on which they appeared were too expensive to be called souvenirs, but performed the same function. Some were sold at Spas like Cheltenham and carried a view of the town, and were expensive presents for friends or relatives.

That china ornaments with pictures on them could be produced was the result of the establishment of a British porcelain industry in the middle of the eighteenth century; some people do not realise that the word 'CHINA' means what it says and that for a long time all our porcelain was imported from that country. It was decorated with Chinese landscapes and when the British eventually discovered how to make their own porcelain they continued to decorate it with Chinese designs and landscapes. The first English landscapes were imaginary, and it was not until the end of the century that named English scenes from real life are to be found on china.

Illustrations on pottery articles were somewhat crude, although there are interesting seventeenth century examples, but there is no suggestion that other than utility articles were produced. It was the transfer system of printing designs and pictures on pottery and porcelain that eventually enabled the mass production of china articles with a consequent reduction in cost.

It would be nice if we could say who first produced pictorial souvenirs, and at the moment there are two contenders for the title.

A decorator, William Absolon, working in Lowestoft, produced quite a large number of

3 Eighteenth-century box of pink enamel with lid of white enamel, carrying a black print of a bridge with the words 'A Prefent from the Iron Bridge.' Length 1·7″ (4·3 cm.)

4 Iron Bridge, Shropshire as seen today. This was originally constructed in 1779, using mortice and tenon joints with wedges and dowels. No nuts and bolts were used.

articles with just 'A Trifle from . . .' on them and a few such rare examples with views can be seen in Norwich Museum. At the same time the Bilston Enamellers were producing patch boxes in quantity with transfer prints, many with captions reading 'A Trifle' or 'A Present from . . .'. Others carried greetings and some had black and white or coloured prints of named places accompanied by a caption. Some had a mirror made of steel or glass which enabled the owner to put on a patch which was intended either for effect or for hiding a facial blemish. We have a plain box which still contains some of the original patches. Plate No. 3 shows a box with a print of the Iron Bridge in Shropshire accompanied by a photograph (Plate No. 4) taken in August 1972—nearly two hundred years after the bridge was built.

It would have been thought that these boxes would have remained popular for a long time, especially those which had a view on them, for they covered the spas and other well-known places including the seaside. They were probably relatively expensive and not good enough in quality for the gift trade, and may be at the time there simply was not a big enough market to keep them going. Somehow we have come to regard pictorial souvenirs as inexpensive articles requiring a mass market and such a market did not exist until the population explosion, which occurred with the Industrial Revolution and the arrival of the railways. The Great Exhibition of 1851 could not have been held unless the main trunk lines had been completed and the London and North Western Railway alone is recorded as having carried over 700,000 excursionists on day trips at 5/- (25p) per head. This is the material on which souvenirs thrive and the Exhibition marked the establishment of a trend which has continued ever since. It matters not whether news of events are referred to as Commemorata or as souvenirs, but as over six million visitors came to the Exhibition there must have been a great quantity sold on this occasion of which there are some with excellent views (see Plates Nos. 66 and 67).

5 Saucer with gilded rim and an overglaze black print of 'Llangollen from the Railway Station'.
Unmarked.   Diam.   5·4″ (13·7 cm.)

From early in the nineteenth century the scenes which interested people sufficiently to illustrate on a gift or souvenir were Cathedrals, Castles, ruins of Castles and Abbeys, tourist attractions such as Stonehenge, Stratford-on-Avon and above all, London. Right up to the time of the first foreign imports in the 1880s you may expect to find examples, all British made, with excellent transfer prints of views. After 1880 every seaside resort, every city, every tourist resort and many a remote hamlet had its memorial made either by British or foreign manufacturers. That this phase was to last just over thirty years and never to reach the same proportions after the First World War, makes this period 1880–1914 so worthwhile to study.

As each place became a candidate for a souvenir, some were better endowed with interesting features than others, and so we see numbers of churches, and in the cities 'The New Town Hall' or 'Art Gallery' or even 'Post Office', all of them quite impressive in their day. Equally impressive must have been the opening of the Railway Station, the gateway to freedom for many, but it is scenes such as in Plate No. 5 which are so fascinating. The passengers are standing in the open at Llangollen waiting for the approaching train on the original broad gauge railway. Today the railway has gone, leaving the canal which had been built long before it, to enjoy a new form of use as a pleasure waterway.

A curious extension of the use of a view is the washstand set shown in Plate No. 6. It carries the mark of a retailer, 'C. Burt, Swanage', and the print has been attributed to one of a series of local views published in 1858. Hardly a souvenir to be taken home from a place that had no rail communication until a later date, but maybe a special commission for a large house or even hotel.

6 Toilet set with seven similar underglaze black prints of 'Swanage from Peveril Point'. Unmarked (English). Dealer's mark: C. Burt, Swanage. Height of jug 12·6″ (32·00 cm.)

There has been little change in the physical appearance of many places but sixty or seventy years ago the streets were not jammed with cars and the horse was still supreme, and we are even able to see a horsedrawn traffic jam on London Bridge. The automobile had clearly made little impression for it is only recorded properly in Plate No. 118 at Maidstone around 1900; a car appears in the scene in Plate No. 164 in front of St Paul's, and in Plate No. 17 the charabanc or omnibus makes its first appearance on the front at Weston-super-Mare. If the street scene has changed so has the dress and habits of the people, particularly at the seaside, and any piece which has a picture depicting the social scene is well worth acquiring. Such items provoke enquiry and it is for this reason that in illustrating our collection we have thought it worthwhile to give a brief history of the spas, seaside resorts or tourist attractions. Quite apart from finding out its place in history it is worthwhile visiting and maybe photographing the same scene today. We have, for example, taken pictures of London Bridge being dismantled stone by stone and the building of the new London Bridge. One day we may even visit the old bridge in its new home in Arizona. Always take the souvenir with you. It helps when making enquiries and acts as a passport to further knowledge.

In the meantime another form of picture had begun to appear—the photograph—which was first developed in Britain by Fox Talbot in the 1840s. By the time of the Crimean War in 1856, Fenton was sent out there with the first wartime camera unit. Later, the first postcards appeared which in due course took full advantage of this new medium, extending their sales and being complementary to the sales of pictorial souvenirs, so much so that in the end postcards probably did more to destroy the demand for souvenirs than any other factor. Nevertheless, photographs played a necessary part in providing the pictures from which the transfer prints were made for souvenirs and the Germans used a photographic transfer process which, with colour tinting, was very effective.

3 The Spas

The word 'Spa' comes from the Belgian town of that name which was founded as a resort as long ago as 1326 and, like a number of other chalybeate springs on the Continent, was famous long before the British started looking for them at home. It was the returning Cavalier exiles who brought with them the idea of organised spas on Continental standards. What the British had to find had already begun life as holy wells where the combination of a saint and the water were said to answer the prayers of those requiring a cure to their ailments. The Reformation, however, did away with the saints and the wells became wishing wells. The power and mystique of the wells declined, until, that is, the idea of drinking the water instead came in. It was not the wells with the clearest pure water which were sought after but those which were heavy and coloured, and these had a pretty unpleasant smell. There was no reliable analysis of water until well into the nineteenth century, and the doctors vied with each other in promoting the healing qualities of their favourite spa. With the establishment of the spas, these towns were to enjoy a social predominance which was to last throughout the eighteenth century and was only to decline with the advent of the seaside watering places. Their social decline was subsequently replaced by a proper scientific assessment of the healing properties of their waters and as towns they continued to flourish, eventually becoming inland pleasure resorts.

What must interest us is the reference that has already been made on page 13 to the sale of souvenirs at Tunbridge Wells in 1766. All the Spas must have had a gift trade and Tunbridge was able to provide its own wooden ware, although it was too early for pictures. There are patch boxes with miniature pictures of Bath, Harrogate and Tunbridge, but for the early ceramic views of spas like Cheltenham, Malvern and Bath we have to look at the ornamental gifts provided by firms like Worcester and Coalport, which were too expensive to be classed as true souvenirs. Whatever you may like to call them, the big Spas have always maintained a gift and souvenir trade from their earliest beginning and time may bring to light many more pictorial souvenirs both English and Continental, for spas were certainly not neglected as a market by the foreign manufacturers.

7 Pink fluted teapot with rectangular black overglaze print of Bath
 Abbey. Mark: 'Made in Bohemia', printed overglaze in a circle.
 Height 4·8″ (12·2 cm.)

Bath was a spa in the days of the Romans—Aquae Sulis as they called it. Their Great Bath,
73′ long with dressing rooms and a gallery, attracted invalids from Europe and was used by the
Roman soldiers who occupied Britain. When the Romans left in 410 A.D. the baths appear to
have fallen into disuse. It is not until the sixteenth century that we again hear of 'The Hot
Bath' being used by sufferers from leprosy and other maladies.

In the eighteenth century the Roman Baths were rediscovered and the hot springs which bubble
up at a temperature of 120°F attracted more and more people to 'take the cure'. Bath became
fashionable. A local builder, John Wood, who had worked for some years in London and the
north, returned to his native city and began a 'building development'. He planned and designed
Gay Street (1727), Queen Square (1729–36), the Circus (1754) and the mansion of Prior Park
(1735–48). His son, John Wood the Younger, continued the work after his father's death in 1754,
designing the Royal Crescent (1767–75), the New Assembly Rooms (1769–71) and the Hot Bath
(1773–7)—later to become the Old Royal Baths.

Throughout the period from 1705 to 1745 Bath owed much to the popularity of one man, Beau
Nash, who established the Assembly Rooms and laid down a code of etiquette and dress. The
popularity of the spa continued; it was a magnet for all the colourful, fashionable, literary and
artistic characters of the Kingdom. In the nineteenth century the spa lost much of its former
grandeur but continued to attract many invalids and retired people.

Apart from the fine Georgian architecture, the city boasts an Abbey Church which dates
mainly from the Stuart period. This appears frequently on Bath souvenirs of the 1880–1914
period.

8a (*left*) Cup (c. 1880) with underglaze black prints of 'The Pavilion, Buxton' on one side and 'The Palace Hotel, Buxton' on the other. Gilded rim. Unmarked but probably of Staffordshire origin. Height 2·6″ (6·7 cm.)

8b (*right*) Saucer (c. 1880) with underglaze black print of 'Devonshire Hospital, Buxton'. Gilded rim. Unmarked. Diam. 5·4″ (13·7 cm.)

The thermal and chalybeate springs of Buxton were known to the Romans but its development as a spa dates mainly from late in the eighteenth century. The main spring is St Anne's Well with a temperature of over 80°F and the waters were said to be 'specially valuable in chronic gouty and rheumatic affections'. The main developments have been carried out by the Dukes of Devonshire. The fifth duke virtually rebuilt the town and brought in John Carr of York to design the new buildings. The Crescent, designed in the Doric style, was begun in 1780 and cost the Duke £120,000. In 1784 the first ball was held in the Crescent Ballroom at the Great Hotel. The Crescent was the nucleus of modern Buxton. Carr next built the 'Great Stables' behind the Crescent to house three hundred horses, vehicles, coachmen and grooms.

The next stage of development came in the second half of the nineteenth century, stimulated by the arrival of the railway in 1863. The Great Stables had already been adapted to take patients and became the Devonshire Royal Hospital in 1857. The area in front of the new hospital was laid out with 'ornamental gardens, with a handsome pavilion, central hall, conservatories and concert hall'. In 1868 the Palace Hotel was built in the Italian style, near the new railway station. By 1880 the conversion of the Great Stables into the Devonshire Hospital had been completed, Buxton was a 'going concern', now largely independent of its landlord and the population was growing; from just over 6,000 in 1881 it rose to over 10,000 by 1901. This was the period when souvenirs of Buxton were made and sold in large numbers.

9a (*left*) Vase with overglaze tinted print of Droitwich showing a street scene with cyclist and a building carrying an advertisement for 'Super Cycles, Coventry'. The print is framed in a gilt band, there is gilding on the handles and rim, and the upper part of the vase has been sprayed with blue enamel. Unmarked. (Foreign) Height 5·7″ (14·5 cm.)

9b (*right*) Porcelain plate with an underglaze black print of the 'Sulphur Well, Harrogate' enclosed in a wreath of leaves. Underglaze mark 'C. Fortune, China Dealer, Harrogate' on a ribbon, printed in black. (English). Diam. 6″ (15·2 cm.)

The salt springs of Droitwich, the Roman Salinae, have been used for centuries but largely for the commercial production of salt. The Royal Baths were opened in 1836 and from this date the town could be called a spa. These are supplied with 'water equivalent in saltness to about seven times the strength of seawater, and is of efficacy in cases of gout, rheumatism, sciatica and dyspepsia'.

Harrogate has had a reputation for medicinal waters since 1770; saline and sulphur springs 'abound in the town by dozens'. An Act of Parliament of 1770 refers to the wells at Harrogate 'to which during the summer season great numbers of persons constantly resort'. These patients were asked by their doctors to lie down in coffin-shaped tubs. William Addison in his *English Spas* (1951) quotes a poem of 1811:

> Astonished I was when I came to my doffing,
> A tub of hot water made just like a coffin,
> In which the good woman who attended the bath,
> Declar'd I must lie down as straight as a lath,
> Just keeping my face above water, that so
> I might better inhale the fumes from below

More up to date establishments followed—the Victorian Baths (1832), the Royal Chalybeate Spa (1835), the Royal Pump Room (1834), the new Victoria Baths (1871); the old Sulphur Well (seen on a souvenir plate) in its cupola building is now enclosed in the Bogs Valley Gardens which were opened in 1887.

10a (*left*) Mug with black overglaze print of the 'Abbey Church, Great Malvern'. Gilding on rim, base and handle. Unmarked, but 'feathering' on handle indicates Worcester. Height 4·6″ (11·7 cm.)
10b (*right*) Small mug with view of 'The Parades, Leamington'. Unmarked, but also Worcester. Height 2·9″ (7·4 cm.)

The possibility that Great Malvern might become a fashionable spa was realised in the middle of the eighteenth century by a Worcester doctor, John Wall, who was also involved in founding the porcelain factory at Worcester. He had some difficulty, however, in convincing people that the water had curative properties because, unlike the water of other spas which was unpleasant to take, people took pleasure in drinking the Malvern water which was pure and fresh. Indeed, a chemical analysis proved its purity and Dr Wall was the subject of some ridicule:

'The Malvern water,' says Dr Wall,
'Is famed for containing nothing at all'.

However, he persevered. He practised at Malvern for eighteen years and had some success. But the real possibilities were not fully exploited until the middle of the nineteenth century when a Dr James Wilson set up a hydropathic practice. Two other doctors followed suit—Dr J. M. Gully and Dr E. B. Grindrod. The spa flourished, attracting such visitors as Carlyle, Dickens, Gladstone, Tennyson and Florence Nightingale. However, by about 1880, Wilson and Gully had died and Grindrod had left the town. The hydropathic centres became hotels and Malvern died as a spa, though it found other attractions for visitors as a festival and conference centre. 'Malvern Water' is now being sold as a 'table' water.

Leamington had a population of 315 in 1807, when the saline springs had already begun to attract attention. In Regency days it developed rapidly after the Victoria Bridge across the Leam was opened in 1809. The Prince Regent stayed in the town in 1819 and Queen Victoria in 1838, after which it became a favourite Victorian resort. The Lower Parade has the Royal Leamington Baths and nearby are the Jephson Gardens, named after a doctor who worked hard to establish the town's reputation.

The view of the 'Parade' on the mug (above) is also seen on marked Worcester cups and saucers dated 1873.

11a (*left*) Porcelain saucer with overglaze black print of 'High Tor, Matlock'. Unmarked (Staffordshire). Diam. 5·3″ (13·5 cm.)
11b (*right*) Porcelain cup with overglaze black print of 'Derwent Parade, Matlock'. Unmarked (Staffordshire). Height 2·6″ (6·6 cm.)

Matlock Bath on the River Derwent has medicinal springs which were used in the seventeenth century. It owes its popularity as a spa partly to its situation in the limestone country of the southern Pennines and partly to Dr John Smedley, a local mill owner who denounced doctors and Church of England parsons, preaching the merits of hydropathy and non-conformism. Between 1853 and 1874 he established the largest hydropathic institution in the country— 'Smedley's Hydro' as it was called.

The springs come from the limestone rock and as they pour over objects placed in the water a calcareous deposit forms and the objects are 'petrified'. There are many caves in the district and the river Derwent flows through a narrow gorge where limestone crags, of which the most notable is High Tor (673′), rise above the wooded slopes. Matlock has, therefore, become a holiday centre as well as a spa.

Souvenirs of Matlock include not only the pictorial wares shown above but 'petrified' birds' nests, plants and other objects and all manner of vases, paperweights and trinkets carved from 'Blue John', an attractive purple-blue substance found in the local rocks.

12 Mug with overglaze black print of the 'Pump Room and Baths' Tenbury Wells. Rim enamelled in green. Dealer's mark: M. Scragg, Tenbury. (Staffordshire). Height 4″ (10·2 cm.)

13 The Pump Room and Bath, Tenbury Wells, 1971.

The small Worcestershire town of Tenbury Wells is on the River Teme, close to the boundary with Shropshire. It first became famous in 1839 when a mineral well was discovered (33′ below ground), quite accidentally, during a search for a household water supply. A second well was found in 1840. Baths and a pump room were built and a rosy future for the spa seemed certain. Dr Granville, an authority on hydropathy, said in the 1840's, 'No place is more calculated to be a second Leamington than this very Tenbury. Neither is there in any part of England a mineral water which, when properly managed, is likely to acquire a greater reputation.' However, development took a different course. Tenbury became a spa for the middle and poorer classes, then declined and only revived again shortly before the First World War, after the baths had been renovated and modernised. The Tenbury Baths Company which, incidentally, persuaded the railway and the post office to add the 'Wells' to the name of Tenbury, issued its own publicity:

'Tenbury Spa is designed for the middle classes, for those people who deserve a cure, as effective as any, yet as cheaply as possible. In the form of a hot bath the Tenbury water is of tremendous value in all cases of Rheumatism, Gout, and all those nervous diseases of the muscles which are generally embraced under the inclusive term of Paralysis. Taken internally the waters claim first attention in their power to overcome Constipation and in all cases of inactivity in this direction will work wonders.'

A local journal of 1911 gave its own review of the waters:

'The Tenbury Waters do not taste at all bad—there is certainly no need to hold the nose, as is the case with the sulphuretted hydrogen waters of Harrogate and Strathpeffer.'

Nevertheless, this 'town in the orchard', as it was called, continued to survive largely as a market town, serving the hop and fruit growing area around.

14a *(left)* Red porcelain plate with gilded rim and a black print of 'Tunbridge Wells from the Common'. Unmarked. (Foreign) Diam. 7·9″ (20 cm.)

14b *(right)* Bowl with gilded rim and tinted print of 'Tunbridge Wells from the Common'. Mark 'Made in Germany' within concentric circles. Height 2·5″ (6·3 cm.)

The medicinal qualities of the chalybeate springs of Tunbridge Wells were recognised in 1606 by Lord North. Shortly afterwards the Earl of Abergavenny enclosed two springs and the 'Spa' was established. In 1630 Queen Henrietta, wife of Charles I, attended with a large suite. Accommodation could not keep pace with demand and for many years some of the visitors had to resort to tents. This was remedied by the end of the seventeenth century and the town became a fashionable resort. It was often visited by Catherine of Braganza, wife of Charles II. By 1700, tiles had been laid along the part of the town near the springs, now known as 'The Pantiles', and in the eighteenth century many eminent visitors came from London—Colley Cibber, the actor and dramatist, Dr Johnson, David Garrick, Samuel Richardson the novelist, Sir Joshua Reynolds and Mrs Thrale. Development continued. The Pump Room, a large red-brick building at the south end of the Pantiles, was erected in 1877. It included a large room with a fountain and drawing rooms furnished with the daily papers.

The Common from which these souvenir pictures were taken covered an area of 179 acres and was almost surrounded by the town.

Reference has already been made in Chapter 2 to the old-established business of souvenir wood ware manufacture in the town, those inlaid with mosaic being known as Tunbridge Ware.

4 The Seaside

As a seafaring nation it took us a long time to obtain any real enjoyment from visiting the seaside and to start with it was the enterprising doctors who first promoted the idea that seawater could be used both externally and internally as a cure. Just as the various Spas claimed that their particular waters could cure practically every known disease, so enthusiastic medical propaganda established the seaside watering place as a rival to the inland spas. It adopted from the beginning the same social facilities as the spas with a master of ceremonies, assembly rooms, theatres, libraries, etc., until, with the final achievement of Royal patronage at the end of the eighteenth century, the watering place became socially superior to the spas.

Dr Wittie of Scarborough published a book in 1660 recommending not only bathing in the sea, but also the drinking of seawater as an alternative to spa water which, as luck would have it, was also available at Scarborough, a resort which had the best of both worlds. In 1752 Dr Richard Russell of Lewes published his *Dissertation on the Use of Sea-Water* and two years later moved to Brighton. With the subsequent visit of the Prince Regent in 1783 and the building of his Pavilion, this resort was established together with Weymouth, Southend, Ramsgate and Margate as a fashionable place patronised by Royalty.

15 Monks Rock, Tenby, South Wales, in 1815, showing an early bathing box with canopy. From Middimans' *Select Views of Great Britain*, 1812.

16 Drawing by George Cruickshank of bathing at Brighton in Regency days.

The social aspect was to be completely changed by the arrival of the railways and with it the whole character of the resorts. From the day when railway travel established easy accessibility, rapid growth commenced. The number of annual visitors increased rapidly, the accent changed from health resort to holiday resort and the latter required amusement and entertainment and the facilities to provide it. Some of these facilities were already there, and they were gradually adapted to meet these new circumstances. The main attraction was the sea and in order to enter it a bathing machine had been invented in 1753 by Benjamin Beale of Margate. This was a wooden hut on wheels which was drawn in and out of the water by a horse, during which operation the occupants undressed, bathed and then dressed. Plate No. 15 shows a bathing box at Tenby in South Wales with the canopy used in earlier years to shield the bathers from prying eyes.

As a form of flannel bathing dress, together with worsted stockings, was the recommended wear, it does not seem that much of the human figure was revealed in any case. Bathing, however, was undertaken as a health cure and custom had decreed that it should be undertaken between the hours of 6.00 a.m. and 9.00 a.m. Before long the whole routine was organised by teams of women attendants whose job it was to immerse their unfortunate clients properly, and Plate 16 gives us an idea of how they went about it.

This nasty, uncomfortable, early morning custom went on for generations and it is hardly surprising that bathing and swimming for pleasure took such a long time to come in. The bathing machines began to lose their popularity in the last quarter of the nineteenth century and looking at old photographs reveals that the horses get fewer and the boxes are drawn further up the beach to be used as changing huts.

The souvenir (Plate No. 17) of a model Bathing Box has on the reverse side the caption 'Morning dip 7.30 a.m.' The view of Weston-super-Mare includes what was known as a char-a-banc, the earliest form of omnibus with seats running the whole width of the body and doors to each

27

17 Model Bathing Box with lady emerging. The roof bears an over-glaze black print of 'The Grand Pier, Weston-super-Mare'. Height 3·7″ (9·5 cm.)

row from both sides of the body. This dates the souvenir to some fifty or sixty years ago and the lady as being a little before her time! The souvenir in Plate No. 18 shows that the horses have almost gone and the bathing boxes are drawn up in rows at the top of the beach. Any souvenirs which show these Boxes are of interest, but they generally appear rather indistinctly in the background.

18 Wooden box with views of Isle of Man.

For those who did not fancy the sea bathing prescribed for them, an alternative appeared in the form of Hot and Cold sea baths. Plate No. 37 shows them conveniently situated at the pier head at Clacton.

'The Sands and Railway Station, Ramsgate' (Plate No. 19) is a splendid detailed scene and deserves close study. The ladies are all wearing crinolines which had been in fashion since the 1820's, reached their maximum point of expansion during the 1860's, and then reduced again in

19 Saucer with underglaze print in black of the 'Sands & Railway Station, Ramsgate'. Unmarked (English). Diam. 5·3″ (13·5 cm.)

size to more manageable proportions. As the railway arrived in 1863, we date this scene as being not long after its arrival; the entertainment is provided by a Minstrel Band, a Punch and Judy show and beyond that a team of acrobats are standing three high. The Bathing Boxes are in the water but, apart from minimal paddling by the children, no one else is interested in the sea. By chance we are able to show exactly the same view in a photograph taken in 1895 (Plate 20) and again in a postcard of 1904 (Plate No. 21).

By the 1890's the crinoline had disappeared and the bustle had taken its place together with a new feature, the parasol, to provide protection from the sun, for it was not until the First World War that the cult of the open air and the exposure of the body to the elements came in and transformed the beach scene. Until then the men all wore hats, often carried a stick, and the children were equally overdressed; but comfort was on the way, upright chairs were being provided as can be seen and the deck chair was shortly to follow (Plate No. 22). If the weather was hot, life on a Victorian or Edwardian beach cannot have been all that comfortable, even with the help of a deck chair to relax in.

20 'A Lively View of the Sands' at Ramsgate from a publication of 1895.

21 A postcard of 'The Sands, Ramsgate' of 1904 on which the sender wrote, 'don't you think this beach is packed!'

22 Ribbon plate with tinted overglaze print of the 'Pier and Promenade and Grandstand' and 'A Present from Eastbourne'. Mark: 'Foreign' printed in green (Schumann). Diam. 7″ (17·8 cm.)

When it comes to the actual use of the sea for swimming we have not seen a single souvenir showing it. In the photographs of this era, one only sees people paddling without shoes and stockings, and the men with trousers rolled up. When sea bathing actually took place the sexes were carefully segregated until we begin to hear the expression 'mixed bathing', and as the horse and his box went out the sexes were allowed to enter the sea in company with each other.

The next facility which was required at a resort was living accommodation and for the mass of holiday makers this was provided by the famous British boarding house, the source of much music hall humour. For the wealthy huge hotels were put up at all the leading resorts, so solidly built that they not only survive today but, now modernised, will be with us for a long time yet. Plate No. 23 shows the Grand Hotel, Brighton, over a hundred years ago with ladies in crinolines standing at the entrance, and there are many souvenirs of a later date showing hotels and providing a little advertising as well, whilst the boarding house remains unremembered.

One of the main features in any resort, and for which there was always a souvenir, was the Pier and so popular did they become that the bigger places had two. The Chain Pier at Brighton, long since demolished, was the first in this country and had the distinction of having been painted by Constable from one side and by Turner from the other; but souvenirs showing that pier are rare. At the end of the pier it was usual to erect a theatre or music hall on the superstructure. Some piers were so long that an additional attraction was provided by running a miniature railway to the end. The piers were an essential part of the entertainment provided by a resort and were reinforced by such things as Big Wheels and Towers, such as the one at Blackpool modelled on

23 Porcelain mug with maroon rim and an underglaze black print of
the 'Grand Hotel, Brighton'. Unmarked (English). Height: 3·3″
(8·4 cm.)

the Eiffel Tower (Plate No. 24). Aquariums were also equally popular. All these features were
commemorated by souvenirs.

The period which was to see the great development of the seaside was also to see the British
lead the world in all sorts of sporting activities. Our souvenirs will show us sailing ships, soon to
disappear, still in all the ports, but beach scenes show that there was already much sailing activity
and its popularity continued to grow. By the 1890's golf courses were springing up everywhere
and every seaside resort found it necessary to build one. Plate No. 25 shows two plates with
delightful illustrations of the golfing dress of the time. The clubs have 'fat' handles and the two
handed grip that was then used can be noted. Another, perhaps more definite, souvenir can be
seen in Plate No. 114, where we have an example of golfing humour—and if anyone doubts its
suitability to the times, let us quote the opening sentence of Chapter 15 of *Golf* (Badminton
Series, 1892) by A. J. Balfour, M.P., a future Prime Minister: 'Gradually round all the great
games there collects a body of sentiment and tradition unknown to or despised by a profane
public, but dear to their votaries, and forming a common bond of union among those who
practise their rites.' It is nice to have a souvenir, pictorial at that.

The heyday for pictorial souvenirs was between 1880–1914 and, of all those produced, at least
half relate to the seaside; we are indebted to an album of pictures of the chief seaside places of
interest in Great Britain entitled *Round the Coast* published by George Newnes in 1895, and the
introduction is perhaps worth quoting in full:

'We have not the least hesitation in placing this work before the English speaking world, knowing full well that it would be almost impossible to find, throughout the length and breadth of our
peerless Empire a solitary individual who is wholly unacquainted with Margate, Brighton and
Scarborough. We love our haunts by the sea; the poorest amongst us regards his favourite resort
pretty much as a rich man does his country seat—as a place of relaxation from the hurley burley

24 Cup and saucer with underglaze black prints respectively of 'The Wheel, Blackpool' and 'Blackpool Tower & Wheel'. Unmarked (English). Diam. of saucer 5·5″ (14·0 cm.)

25 Plates (Minton mark of 1901) with underglaze prints of golfers with the monogram of the artist—W.S.

of life and yet a home withal. Therefore we asseverate—and that without fear of contradiction—that it would be impossible to place upon the table in a British household a more interesting souvenir of happy days than this volume. It requires no great effort of the imagination to picture a few friends of long standing glancing through this work. How the eyes brighten at the sight of a familiar spot and how vividly the old associations crowd back to the mind memories of glowing careless days, that gave new life to the jaded worker, and caused the brain weary to forget their ineffable TAEDIUM VITAE.'

In this spirit let us look at some of the souvenirs sold in 'these haunts by the sea' and a little more closely at their development. Quotations are from the book mentioned above or other similar publications of the period. As each resort had a large range of souvenirs supplied by different manufacturers both British and foreign, it will be appreciated that only a representative selection of pieces can be illustrated and from only a limited number of resorts.

26 (*left*) Saucer with underglaze print of the 'North Shore' within a gilded circle. Unmarked but Staffordshire. Diam. 5·4″ (13·7 cm.)

27 (*right*) Teapot in pink and white with an overglaze print of the 'South Pier' touched up with yellow enamel. Mark: MADE IN GERMANY within concentric circles, the whole printed overglaze in reddish-brown. A second mark shows an open hand in the same colour. Height 5″ (12·7 cm.)

In 1750 Blackpool was little more than a hamlet but by the end of the eighteenth century it had already become a small resort with a parade, bowling greens and other attractions, catering for the manufacturers of Bolton and Manchester, and the merchants of Liverpool. Bathing was already popular but the sexes were segregated. The gentlemen had the first 'go' and then, when a bell was rung, the ladies assembled and the gentlemen discreetly disappeared.

Development was steady and accelerated towards the end of the nineteenth century. A long marine parade and carriage drive were built and steadily extended and by 1895 there were two piers. 'Both the piers are large; the north one is more select, and the south the more popular—just as a penny pier where dancing goes on all day in summer. In this Lancashire watering place there are theatres, a 'Grand Opera House', numerous concert halls, an aquarium, a circus, a menagerie, fine winter gardens and other places of public assemblies where concerts, fireworks, and all sorts of entertainments will be found duly provided. The promenade is lighted by electricity and has an electric tramway. Not to be left behind in any respect Blackpool now has an Eiffel Tower of its own, which looks down upon a busy scene of enjoyment that suggests a fair rather than a seaside resort.'

28 (*left*) Ribbon plate heavily gilded with tinted overglaze view of the 'Pier and Sands' and the words 'A Present from Bognor'. Schumann mark. Diam. 7·1″ (18 cm.)

29 (*right*) Cruet in the shape of a pair of binoculars with overglaze prints of 'The Pier' and the 'West Promenade and Sands'. Unmarked (Foreign). Height 2·9″ (7·4 cm.)

The early development of Bognor was due to the enterprise of one man. 'About 1785 Sir Richard Hotham, a wealthy Southwark hatter, who determined on acquiring the glory of a seaside Romulus, set to work to erect a town of first-class villas in this pleasant spot, with a view to creating a truly *recherché* watering-place to be known to posterity as Hothampton. He spent £60,000; he erected and furnished some really commodious villas, but did not succeed in giving his name to his own creation.' Nevertheless, there is today a 'Hotham Place' in Bognor.

Some thirty years later attention was drawn to the town when Princess Charlotte, only child of George, Prince of Wales (later George IV) chose Bognor for a course of sea-bathing she was ordered by her doctor. She stayed at Downe House and drove about the district in a cart drawn by four grey ponies, rambled over the heath and bathed three or four times a week. From this time Bognor developed as most other resorts. A sea-wall and esplanade were built and a pier 1,000′ in length.

Immediately to the east of Bognor is Felpham, which also helped to spread the fame of this stretch of coast. Here lived William Hayley (1745–1820), the poet, and it was to illustrate his ballads that William Blake (1757–1827) came to the village. In summer Mrs Amelia Opie (1769–1853), the novelist, came to stay with Hayley and the presence of these celebrities attracted a good deal of attention.

The town became Bognor Regis after George V's convalescence there in 1934.

36

30a (left) Saucer with black underglaze print of 'The Gardens'.
Dealer's mark: Manufactured for J. F. Bell, Bournemouth 'Fancy
Fair.' (English). Diam. 5·6" (14·2 cm.)

30b (right) Hotwater jug (c. 1920–30) with underglaze tinted print of
East Cliff. Mark: 'Victoria Czechoslovakia' printed overglaze.
Height 6" (15·2 cm.)

Bournemouth is a resort which has grown very rapidly. About 150 years ago it hardly existed.
By 1830 there were a few private houses and a few cottages on the sandy heathland on which the
town now stands, which stretched from the Hampshire settlement of Christchurch to the Dorset
port of Poole. It was developed as a resort by Sir George Gervis, who thought that every house
should stand in its own grounds and that all should have a different appearance. They were
mainly copies of Greek or Italian styles or were early expressions of Victorian gothic revival.
Pines of many kinds were planted around them and today it is possible to identify the Scots pine,
Black Austrian pine, Corsican pine and Monterey pine in the urban landscape. The need to
keep the resort 'select' was urged vigorously by Dr Granville, who publicized the health-giving
qualities of the air, the sea, and the 'balsamic effluvia' of the pines. As a result many invalids,
especially consumptives, were attracted to Bournemouth which soon became a 'Metropolis of
Bath Chairs'. Many of the other residents found it dull. Robert Louis Stevenson, who lived in
Alum Chine Road from 1884–7, wrote that he lived 'like a weevil in a biscuit'; but by this time
the town was changing rapidly. A pier had been constructed and a sea front extended on either
side—the East Cliff (see jug above) towards Christchurch, the West Cliff towards Poole. In the
1890's public gardens (see saucer above) were laid out along the valley of the Bourne which runs
inland from the pier—'blooming with arbutus, rhododendrons and other choice shrubs, under
the shade of fir trees which clothe its sides'.

31 Moulded cream-and-brown sardine dish printed with a tinted view of the 'Entrance to the Pier, Bournemouth'. The handle of the lid is shaped like a fish. Unmarked, but German. Length 6·3″ (16 cm.)

Bournemouth Pier was built in 1876 and shelters were added at the pierhead in 1885. The need to turn the town into a modern resort, however, did not prevent the earlier snobbery from lingering on. An account of Bournemouth in 1895 points out that 'not a few of the residences are fine mansions standing in extensive and beautiful grounds, which elswhere would rank as country seats. From this select sojourn of delicate ease the working elements of society are for the most part banished to villages and cottages inland and out of sight, so that the town itself, instead of being shut in by shabby suburbs, is at most points fringed by pine woods and moors, its characteristic background.'

Today 'working elements of society' mix with the residents and wealthier visitors. Entertainment of many kinds is provided and the pavilion, built in 1929, can house a symphony orchestra with audiences of 1,500 people. The old bathing machines have become fixtures as bathing huts below the sandy cliffs.

Bournemouth is fused with the adjacent resort of Boscombe which has its own pier (rebuilt since the war), with Southbourne-on-Sea and with Pokesdown. The average visitor is hardly aware of the fact as he passes from one to another, for this stretch of coast has become a single conurbation with well over a quarter of a million people.

32a BROADSTAIRS (*left*) Cup (1860–70) with underglaze print of a
'New View of Broadstairs' and the words 'A Present from Broadstairs'. Unmarked but Staffordshire. Height 2·25″ (5·7 cm.)

32b BRIDLINGTON (*right*) Porcelain mug (c 1900–13) by A. B.
Jones & Sons with overglaze black print of 'Royal Princes Parade'.
Gilded rim. Mark: 'ABJ & SONS' within a Staffordshire knot on a
shield together with the words 'Grafton China, England'. Height
2·7″ (6·9 cm.)

Broadstairs was always a 'modest' resort for family parties, quieter and more select than its larger
and noisier neighbours Margate and Ramsgate. Princess Victoria (later to become Queen) used
to come to Broadstairs each year with her mother on an informal holiday. But the associations
with Dickens are best known. He loved Broadstairs and wrote to a friend 'A good sea, fresh
breezes, fine sand and pleasant walks, with all manner of fishing boats, lighthouses, piers, bathing
machines are its only attractions; but it is one of the freshest and freest places in the world.' Here
in 1839 he wrote part of *Nicholas Nickleby* and in 1849 part of *David Copperfield*.

Bridlington is no mere mushroom watering place, but the harbour of the old town of Bridlington is connected with York by a Roman road. 'The harbour possesses two stone piers from which a
good view can be obtained of the Flamborough Head and will hold about 200 vessels. It is the
only one between Leith and Harwich which can be entered during northerly gales, the Bay
sheltering them until the tide allows entrance. The beach is clean hard sand, and the place
possesses a rather noted chalybeate spring, whose tonic effects in many cases assist those of the
splendidly bracing atmosphere.' Bridlington's sea wall and promenade were built between 1866
and 1869.

33a (*left*) Pink pilgrim bottle with tinted print of 'The Entrance to the Aquarium'. Unmarked (foreign). Height 4·5″ (11·4 cm.)

33b (*centre*) Pink fluted beaker with an oval tinted print of 'Brighton Pier'. Mark: Brown overglaze print—'MADE IN GERMANY' within concentric circles. Height 4·3″ (10·9 cm.)

33c (*right*) Pink mug with tinted print of 'Old Steine, Brighton'. On either side of the print are gilded leaves. Mark 'MADE IN GERMANY' beneath the mark of Unger & Schilde. Height 2·6″ (6·5 cm.)

Brighton, originally known as Brighthelmstone, began as a small fishing village. The man who was responsible for turning it into a fashionable watering place was Dr Richard Russell of Lewes, who in 1752 published a *Dissertation on the Use of Sea-Water*. This stressed the value of drinking sea water and of immersing the body in it. In 1754 Dr Russell built a house in Brighton on the site now occupied by the Royal Albion Hotel, Old Steine, so that he could direct the treatment of his patients. Bathing became popular. Women known as dippers stood fully clothed in the water close to the bathing machines and when the bathers descended to the water took them forcibly by the hand and immersed them. The proper treatment was thus enforced. Many of the dippers became well-known characters. Martha Gunn, for example, who later became 'Beach Attendant', is commemorated in jugs of the period moulded in her likeness like Toby Jugs.

In 1783 the Prince Regent visited Brighton, was delighted with it, and in 1784 commissioned Henry Holland to build the famous Pavilion. It was drastically remodelled by John Nash between 1815 and 1823 to become the 'notorious and eccentric Pavilion' later acquired by the Brighton Commissioners.

The Pavilion added to the popularity of Brighton as a resort. In 1823 a chain pier (later replaced by the Palace Pier) was completed. It consisted of four sets of oak piles driven into the rock, on each of which a pyramided tower of cast iron was erected. These carried the supporting chains. Each tower housed some small shop or amusement. John Gapp, a well-known silhouettist, worked in one of these booths for some twelve years, cutting likenesses from black paper for the visitors.

34 (*above*) Two-handled pink plate with view of the 'West Pier, Brighton', enclosed in a gilt circle. Mark: 'Made in Germany' printed in green. Diam. 9·4″ (23·9 cm.)

35 (*below*) The 'West Pier' today.

In 1841 Brighton was linked by rail to London and cheap excursions were run to the resort. It soon became popular with all classes and more and more amusements were provided. The Aquarium (see Plate No. 33a) was opened in 1872. It was also a promenade 'with newspapers, periodicals and the latest telegrams for the use of the visitors. There are forty-one fish tanks arranged in two of the corridors; and the length of the building exceeds 700 ft.'

In 1886, the West Pier (see above) was opened, near to the Grand Hotel (see Plate No. 23) and the front was crowded with pedestrians, bath chairs, little carts for children drawn by goats, horses and carriages. An account of 1895 states, 'You can hardly walk on the Parade on a fine afternoon without meeting troops of fair horsewomen, attended by their riding masters, sweeping along towards the Downs. The stream of carriages is almost as incessant as on a Drawing Room day at Buckingham Palace. Bands are playing everywhere you go . . .'

36a BUDE (*left*) Moulded basket with overglaze black print of 'Bude Harbour' with sailing ships. The edge carries a deep band of gilding. Unmarked (foreign). Height 4·5″ (11·4 cm.)

36b BUDLEIGH SALTERTON (*right*) Teapot in grey and white with an oval print of 'Budleigh Salterton—East View' within a gilt line. Unmarked (foreign). Height 4·5″ (11·4 cm.)

As a small seaport on the north coast of Cornwall, Bude had a harbour long before it developed as a resort, which had to await the arrival of the railway. The anchorage was used by vessels up to 300 tons and was protected by a breakwater some 900′ long. The chief export was the local sand, which contains a high percentage of lime and has always been in demand as a dressing for farmland. However, the chief attraction for visitors lay in the rugged sea cliffs and the golf links rather than in the sands. Bathing presented problems. 'The bathing here is not very good. The tides are too violent for machines, and therefore canvas tents are erected on the sands for the use of bathers, who have to encounter high and heavy billows rolling in from the Atlantic.' (1895).

Budleigh Salterton started as a small South Devon village of cob cottages and when it became a 'watering place' was very conscious of its own exclusiveness. Day trippers were unknown. The nearest station was at Exmouth and the trains were met by an omnibus which ran four times a day. It was described in the 1890's as 'a charming little spot, which, thanks to the absence of the railway, retains much of its primitive simplicity—a characteristic that has chiefly helped to raise it in the estimation of the judicious as a quiet resort, whether in the summer or the winter season.' Yet it was not too proud to sell its pictorial souvenirs.

37*a* Pink tobacco jar with pipe knop. The jar carries an oval tinted print of the 'Pier, Clacton'. Mark: Red print of three stacked rifles with MADE IN GERMANY in straight lines. Mark of Max Emanuel & Co. Height 5·5″ (14 cm.)

37*b* (*right*) Pink vase with a circular tinted print of 'Clacton'. Mark: Red print MADE IN GERMANY in straight lines. Height 5·5″ (14 cm.)

The development of Clacton-on-Sea as a resort was relatively late. A wooden pier was constructed in 1871 and Clyde-built steamers operated daily in summer to Southend (28 miles) and London Bridge (73 miles). One of the problems was coast erosion, because the cliffs were of soft rock. In 1881 a concrete sea wall was built with flights of steps giving access to the sandy beach. Shortly afterwards the railway arrived and real development began. The pier was extended and the numbers of promenaders buying tickets reflect the increasing prosperity of the town. In 1885, 94,032 tickets were sold; by 1889 the number had reached 147,538. In 1895 a report states: 'That Clacton-on-Sea is rapidly becoming a popular resort will be seen from the fact that it numbers amongst its institutions an immense corrugated iron building, with a lawn in front, known as Rigg's Retreat, which will accommodate 1,200 persons at one time.'

Clacton-on-Sea took a great pride in its lifeboat station. When the Prince of Wales returned from India in 1869 he gave £4,000 to the Royal National Lifeboat Institution to found and maintain two stations. Clacton-on-Sea was chosen as one site and the first lifeboat was launched from it in 1878, in the presence of over 10,000 people.

38 Porcelain spill vase with an overglaze black print of a 'View of Cromer'. Dealer's mark: ABEL, Cromer. (English.) Height 4·5″ (11·4 cm.)

'Cromer is becoming every year more fashionable as a summer watering place, chiefly on account of its bracing air and fine beach of firm level sands, some miles in extent.' This statement was written in 1900 but could easily have been written twenty years earlier. Winston Churchill was sent there with his governess in 1885 when he was ten years of age. The list of eminent visitors at this period would be long—Empress Elizabeth of Austria, Compton MacKenzie, Oscar Wilde, J. M. Barrie, Sir Henry Irving, Alfred Tennyson, Lord Curzon, Ellen Terry. One of the reasons that kept it 'select' was the distance from any large centre of population. It was not a place for the day excursionist. In any case the Great Eastern Railway did not come to Cromer until 1876, so it had a late start compared with other resorts. The Midland and Great Northern Railway established a station at Cromer Beach in 1889 and then followed a period of hotel building—The Grand (1890–91), the Metropole (1893–4), the rebuilding of the Hotel de Paris (1894–5) and the Royal Links Hotel (1892–5) close to the golf course. Note that lodging houses do not seem to have developed at the same rate. The esplanade was rebuilt in the 1890's and a pier was opened in 1901. The resort flourished until the First World War, but there was little further development in the 1920's. It still attracts people who like a quieter holiday than they would get in the larger East Anglian resorts nearer London—Great Yarmouth, Clacton and Southend-on-Sea—all much larger, and much noisier.

39 Jug (c 1880) with an overglaze printed view of the 'Grand Parade, Eastbourne' on both sides. Mark: DAVENPORT with an anchor printed in underglaze blue. Also an overglaze dealer's mark: GOSLING, EASTBOURNE. Height 7·8″ (19·8 cm.)

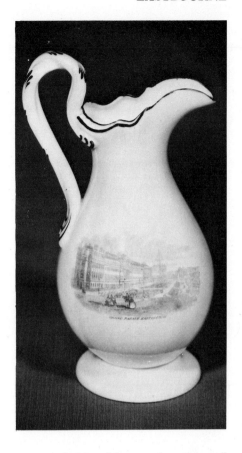

Eastbourne was described at the turn of the century as 'the most fashionable watering-place of Sussex, and perhaps of the South Coast'. Its development began about 1870, when the village of Eastbourne was linked with the hamlets of Southbourne, Sea Houses and Meads. This was carried out under the management of the Duke of Devonshire, the principal ground landlord.

The Grand Parade (see jug above) was planned as 'a beautiful marine treble-terraced walk. It consists of an upper and lower promenade, connected at intervals by flights of steps, the intervening slopes being planted with tamarisks and other shrubs and evergreens.' (The Davenport souvenir china supplied to Gosling's also included cups and saucers with the same view.)

The 1,000′ long pier at Eastbourne (see Plate No. 22) was opened in 1872 and its pavilion and concert hall were added in 1888. Pride of place was strong as the following description (1895) suggests: 'One must mention that there are noble tree-planted streets and shady avenues, an imposing sea-front of about three miles, and excellent beach of mingled sand and shingle, a pier of the most approved pattern, an abundance of seats and shelters, gardens and promenades, and every convenience for bathing, boating and fishing, as well as first-class hotels, well-built houses, tempting shops and irreproachable sanitary arrangements and water supply.'

40a (*left*) two-handled vase with a tinted print of 'Folkestone Harbour'.
Unmarked (foreign). Height 6·2″ (15·7 cm.)
40b (*right*) Similar vase with a tinted print of 'The Lees'.

Unlike some of the larger resorts such as Bournemouth, which was little more than a village two hundred years ago, Folkestone existed as a seaport in the twelfth century. In the latter part of the eighteenth and in the early nineteenth century, the town acquired some notoriety in connection with a contraband trade with France. As a smuggling centre it flourished. In 1809 the harbour was greatly improved under the direction of Thomas Telford (1757–1834) but the major development followed the arrival of the South-Eastern Railway in 1844, when a cross-Channel packet service was established between Folkestone and Boulogne.

Folkestone soon developed as a resort. A promenade pier was built in 1888 and building spread along the coast towards Sandgate 'and the houses here face a grassy promenade called The Lees which extends to the edge of the cliffs and command a fine view of the Channel and the coast of France'. The road beneath the cliff was linked with the Lees by hydraulic lifts as well as footpaths and steps.

Every effort was made to keep Folkestone 'select'. 'The policy of the townspeople is such as to discourage excursionists and seek the patronage of the higher class of visitors; consequently the humours of the sands so conspicuous at Margate or at Yarmouth are hardly to be looked for at Folkestone, where the most exciting pastime is the going and coming of the Channel boats and the landing of their woebegone passengers.' (1895)

41a (*left*) Small moulded reeded jug with a black underglaze print of
'Britannia Pier, Yarmouth'. Gilded rim. Unmarked but Staffordshire. Height 3·5″ (8·9 cm.)

41b (*right*) Small moulded jug with a black underglaze print of 'Yarmouth'. Gilded rim. Unmarked but Staffordshire. Height: 3·4″
(8·6 cm.)

Great Yarmouth has always been a fishing port and has always had a considerable foreign trade,
exporting barley from the arable lands of East Anglia and importing coal and timber. Fish were
cured and salted locally; the barley traffic gave rise to a malting industry, and the fishing industry
itself to the manufacture of ropes and nets. The population was largely, therefore, 'working
class'. The development of Great Yarmouth as a resort came later, especially after the arrival of
the Norwich and Yarmouth Railway in the 1840's.

The town is built on a sand-drift formed at the entrance to the joint estuary of the Rivers
Bure, Yare and Waveney. This drift was added to during the spring by the Easterly winds which
prevail at that time of year. So the beaches everywhere were suitable for bathing and, indeed,
for boating. Rowing boats and sailing boats alike were launched from the sand of the gently
sloping beach. Industrial workers mingled with the visitors and shared the excitement and
activity of the frequent fairs and the market. All this prevented Yarmouth from becoming the
kind of 'select' resort found on the south coast. The town was conscious of this even in the 1890's.
'The usual associations of the Norfolk watering place are with bigness, boisterousness and
joviality unrestrained by any false pride.'

Yarmouth had two piers of which the Britannia Pier, destroyed by fire in 1908 (Plate No. 41a),
was the larger, and also a 'Jetty'. Apart from the bathing and boating from the sands, the golf
links, the esplanade, the theatre, the aquarium and the switchback all provide pleasure and
amusement for visitors. (See also miniature souvenirs, Plates Nos. 149 and 150).

42a (*left*) Ribbon plate with a tinted print of the 'New Bandstand and Promenade'. (Note the cyclists in the foreground.) Mark: GERMANY printed in green script (Schumann). Diam. 7″ (17·8 cm.)

42b (*right*) Jug with a printed view of 'Hastings Castle'. Unmarked (foreign). Height 5·6″ (14·2 cm.)

Hastings Castle stands on the brink of the cliff above the town and 'presents the most striking view to be found in Sussex' (an opinion of 1895). The historic town itself was already an attractive place for residents and visitors when Queen Victoria came to the throne. Louis Napoleon lived at Pelham Cottage in 1840 and Louis Philippe, ex-King of the French, lived for a while at the Victoria Hotel in 1845.

Cassell's Gazetteer of 1900 describes the amenities as follows: 'The pier, opened in 1872, is of iron and wood, 900 ft long and has a large pavilion for amusements, and a landing-stage for steamers. The Albert Memorial, the central point of the town, is a clock-tower 65 ft. high and has a statue of the late Prince Consort. The Alexandra Park is a well-kept pleasure ground of 76 acres. The sea-frontage is nearly three miles long and is lighted with electric lamps almost the whole distance. The staple industry of Hastings is the fishery, which gives employment to a large number of persons dwelling mostly at the east end of the town.'

The western suburb of St Leonards is coupled with Hastings as a 'fashionable place of popular resort'. The nearness of other places of interest—Pevensey, Battle Abbey and Fairlight Glen—has been an added advantage.

43*a* (*centre*) Staffordshire spill jar with black overglaze print of 'Herne Bay' showing a view of the pier from the sea. Retailer's mark: H. WELLARD. Height 4″ (10·2 cm.)

43*b* (*left and right*) Pair of pink candlesticks (c 1900) with black overglaze prints of the 'New Pier'. Unmarked (foreign). Height 4·6″ (10·3 cm.)

Herne Bay first developed as a resort in the 1830's when a group of enterprising business men decided to build hotels and provide amenities. The venture failed but its reputation as a watering place had been established and the advent of the London, Chatham and Dover Railway in 1862 brought increasing numbers of visitors. Coaches provided the link with Canterbury.

Thomas Telford built a wooden pier at Herne Bay in 1832, which was attacked by wood boring insects and had to be replaced by an iron pier in 1873. In 1884 a pavilion was added and at the turn of the century the pier was extended. This was the 'New Pier' shown on the candlesticks above.

The Marine Parade, about a mile long, was laid out with pleasure gardens and a lady presented an elaborate clock tower with Ionic and Corinthian pillars which cost her £4,000.

44a (*left*) Moulded pink jug with an oval overglaze tinted print of 'Excursion steamers at Ilfracombe'. Unmarked (Foreign). Height 4·4″ (11·2 cm.) (See also Plate No. 107.)

44b (*right*) Teapot with overglaze tinted print of 'The Capstone, Ilfracombe'. Printed mark in green—a crown with 'Victoria' and 'Austria' Schmidt. Height 4·5″ (11·4 cm.)

The North Devon market town of Ilfracombe was a flourishing port in the days of Edward III and continued with a fishing and coasting trade well into the nineteenth century. The first pier was built in 1730, partly rebuilt in 1760, enlarged between 1823 and 1829 and finally 'improved' in the 1890's when Ilfracombe had become a flourishing resort. Unlike many south coast watering places it was too rocky to develop for seashore bathing and special arrangements had to be made. A special cove under private ownership, used as early as 1825, was approached by a tunnel, where the fee was paid at a turnstile. 'One passes under the Runnycleaves by a dark tunnel that casts a shade of serious resolve upon the would-be bather, and on the hottest day inspires a shiver, premonitory of the coming plunge. This cavernous entrance opens out into a picturesque cove, containing two walled-in bathing pools for ladies and gentlemen, who may here disport themselves safely on the roughest day.'

Many walks were cut in the rocky hillsides and around Capstone Hill, where a band played in the season. A promenade and Winter Garden were constructed and local excursions were encouraged to Watermouth, Combe Martin, Morthoe and Woolacombe Sands. There were steamer trips to Lundy Island and Clovelly and 'Campbell's Steamers' brought excursionists from as far afield as Bristol.

45 (*above*) Cruet in the form of a lighthouse with a print labelled 'Jersey—La Corbière'. The lid is a pepper pot. In the base are two drawers with apertures above them for spoons. Unmarked (foreign). Height 4·2″ (10·7 cm.)

46 (*below*) The same cruet showing the individual parts.

Jersey, with the other Channel Islands, was an appanage of the Duchy of Normandy, and became a fief of the English Crown at the time of the Norman Conquest. It is nearer to the French coast than to England and the links with France have always been important. French labour has always been used in summer to help harvest the potato crop—the main crop of the island in the nineteenth century—though the export of flowers and tomatoes was already growing at the end of this period.

The tourist trade was also growing. By 1900 some 45,000 visitors came to the Island, about one third of them from France. Railways then ran from St Helier to the little fishing port of Gorey, noted for Mont Orgueil Castle, to St Aubin, the ancient capital, and to La Corbière, noted for its lighthouse built in 1874. The lighthouse rises 59′ above Corbière Rock, which itself rises 70′ above high water mark. At low tide the lighthouse can be reached across a natural red granite causeway.

St Helier, the main port, had an esplanade and a fine harbour with two piers—the Victoria or Southern pier and the Western or Albert Pier. It was the natural centre from which visitors explored the island.

47a (*left*) Moulded bowl with lustred glaze with a tinted print of 'The Parade'. Unmarked (foreign). Height 2·3″ (5·8 cm.)

47b (*right*) Moulded jug with lustred glaze with a print of 'The Pier, Littlehampton'. Unmarked (foreign). Height 4·0″ (10·2 cm.)

Littlehampton lies between Worthing and Bognor at the mouth of the River Arun in West Sussex. It has been a small seaport for centuries; Queen Matilda landed here in 1139. The harbour was originally defended by a small fort, mounting five 68-pounder guns, which lies on the west bank of the river.

Littlehampton became a watering place at the end of the eighteenth century but grew relatively slowly, mainly as a bathing resort as the soil is sandy. The so-called pier is not a pleasure pier as in other resorts, but a wooden jetty. A parade was built on the flat sands and 'the houses stand some way back, and are separated from the sea by a strip of greensward broken with undulations and clumps of furze which make this spot a capital playground'. Boating was also popular, especially on the River Arun. 'Some very pretty scenery may be reached by boat up the river if the tide be studied.'

The town is, of course, a good centre for the exploration of inland Sussex. It lies five miles south of Arundel with its famous Castle, first mentioned in the will of Alfred the Great.

48a (*left*) Cup with black-printed view of 'Rushen Castle, Castletown' and 'Bradda Head, Port Erin'. Unmarked (English). Height 2·5″ (6·3 cm.)

48b (*centre*) Saucer with a print of 'Douglas'. Unmarked (English). Diam. 5·6″ (14·3 cm.) See also Plate No. 103.

48c (*right*) Mug with a black-printed view of 'Ramsey'. Dealer's Mark: BROUGHTON, RAMSEY (English). Height 2·9″ (7·4 cm.)

The Isle of Man began to develop as a holiday resort in the 1820's, when steamers brought an influx of visitors from across the water. The island folk soon saw in this a new source of revenue. Waiters from the newly built hotels and boarding houses assailed the strangers when they left the ship, thrusting their cards at them and persuading them to stay at their establishments. By 1880 Douglas had become a large and growing watering place and by 1900 was visited annually by 300,000 tourists, chiefly from the Midland and Northern counties. 'It possesses a fine line of mail steamers, running daily to and from Liverpool, and in the summer to Fleetwood, Barrow, Glasgow, Dublin and Belfast.' Many of the visitors made Douglas their centre, with the long line of three and four-storey hotels lining the bay, its piers, promenades, horse-drawn carriages and amusements. Other visitors scattered to smaller centres such as Ramsey and Port Erin.

Ramsey was quite different from Douglas but was also served by steamer services from the mainland. 'Steamers usually land their passengers at Queen's Pier, while occasionally at high tides the vessels go right into the harbour.'

In 1847 Ramsey was fortunate in having a visit from Queen Victoria and Prince Albert. A 45′ Albert Tower was built where the Consort stood to view the town. Needless to say, this was to become 'an eminently respectable town, quiet and healthy . . . Horses may be hired, and there are troops of the meekest of meek donkeys for the children . . . The bathing machines and boats are kept on the south shore of this resort, but they may also be had on the north shore if ordered . . . Altogether we have no hesitation in saying that those who regularly patronized more commonplace resorts find Ramsey a charming and wholly novel change therefrom.'

49a (*left*) Plate (c. 1840) with a print of Douglas Harbour. Unmarked (English). Diam. 6·7″ (17 cm.)

49b (*right*) Pink teapot stand with a view of Laxey Wheel. Mark: MADE IN GERMANY within a circle and a letter 'M'. Diam. 6·3″ (16 cm.)

Castleton, once the capital of the island, with the Castle of Rushen close to the harbour, also attracted visitors as did Port Erin. Port Erin was the southern terminus of the Isle of Man Railway. The bay is enclosed by hills with the grand promontory of Bradda Head sheltering from the north winds. This was a resort beloved by naturalists and those fond of boating and walking. Footpaths branched out from the Falcons Nest Hotel over Bradda Head and the hills around.

Laxey, roughly half way between Douglas and Ramsey, was a mining village but became a great day-resort on the island because of the fine scenery in Laxey Glen and the remarkable 'Great Wheel', erected in 1854 to drain water from the lead mines. It is over 217′ in circumference. Visitors were allowed to go over the works which had an annual yield of some 2,500 tons of ore, of which 'three quarters is pure lead, yielding $2\frac{1}{2}$ tons of silver'.

50a (*left*) Moulded pink plate with handles with a tinted print of 'The Jetty'. Mark: MADE IN GERMANY printed in brown. Overall width, including handles, 11″ (28 cm.)

50b (*right*) Pink and white teapot with a black print of 'Newgate Gapway and Bridge, Margate'. Unmarked (Foreign). Height 5·3″ (13·5 cm.)

The wide stretch of fine sand at Margate and its proximity to London made it a resort in the middle of the eighteenth century. It had a large and safe harbour built by John Smeaton in 1774 and the one-masted sloops known as 'Margate Hoys' carried both passengers and provisions for the town. The first steam packet ran from London to Margate in 1815 and the jetty was built in 1854 and extended in 1876. It is 'over a quarter of a mile in length with a hexagonal head about 720′ in circumference, in the centre of which is a pavilion', says a guide book of 1900.

Bathing was already popular in the eighteenth century and Margate regarded itself as highly advanced. As already mentioned, the bathing machines were provided with modesty hoods, designed by a Quaker, Benjamin Beale, 'to preserve the modesty of the female sex'. The machines stood in the water and the young ladies were held to the breakers by lady dippers standing waist-deep in the sea.

Bathing houses were also popular. These were for season ticket holders—rooms where they could wait for a free machine, read the papers, take their salt drinks or regale themselves with tea or coffee.

51a (*left*) Saucer with tinted print of 'The New Lighthouse and Ramsgate Harbour', the rim enamelled overglaze with a buff-coloured lustre. Unmarked (English). Diam. 2·7″ (6·8 cm.)

51b (*right*) Cup with a print of a view of 'West Cliff'. Unmarked (English). Height 2·7″ (6·8 cm.)

The harbour at Ramsgate is protected by two piers of Purbeck and Portland Stone which are favourite promenades and there is a lighthouse on the western pierhead (see above). It was from Ramsgate Harbour that George IV embarked for Hanover in 1821.

The resort has an 'East Cliff' and a 'West Cliff'. Some of the buildings on both cliffs are notable, for their architect was Augustus Welby Pugin (1812–1852), who helped to design the decorations for the Houses of Parliament (1836–7), built a house for himself in 1846 on the West Cliff and also the adjoining St Augustine's Church (he was converted to Catholicism in 1833). On the East Cliff he designed the 'Granville Hotel'.

Storms have always caused anxiety in Ramsgate. 'During storms', states a guide book of 1895, 'the neighbourhood of the dreaded Goodwin Sands affords the all too frequent excitement of a wreck. At these times all Ramsgate is in a commotion, bidding God-speed to the lifeboat and the steam tug with their gallant crews, who are ever ready for their arduous and dangerous duty.' Ramsgate was a slightly higher class resort than Margate in the nineteenth century. We get the clearest view of what it was like in Victorian times from the famous picture by W. P. Frith of 'Ramsgate Sands'. He did the preliminary sketches for this crowded scene during a holiday in 1857. 'The variety of character on Ramsgate Sands attracted me', he writes in *My Autobiography and Reminiscences*. 'All sorts and conditions of men and women were there. Pretty groups of ladies

52 Ribbon plate with tinted overglaze print showing a 'General View
of the Sands'. Unmarked but attributed to Schumann. Diam. 8·3″
(21 cm.)

were to be found, reading, idling, working and unconsciously forming themselves into very
paintable compositions.'

There have always been crowds on Ramsgate Sands, particularly after the arrival of the direct
rail line from London in 1863. Noise has also been a characteristic. Ruth Manning-Sanders, in
her book *Seaside England* (1951), quotes Jane Welsh Carlyle who wrote of Ramsgate in 1861, 'A
brass band plays all through breakfast, and repeats the performance often during the day, and the
brass band is succeeded by a band of Ethiopians, and that again by a band of female fiddlers!
and interspersed with these are individual barrel-organs, individual Scotch bag-pipes, individual
French horns!'

Late Victorian photographs of the sands show the chairs—solid wooden affairs that preceded
the deck chair, donkeys, beach photographers, Punch and Judy shows and the inevitable line of
bathing machines along the water line. (See Plates Nos. 19, 20 and 21.)

53 A pair of fluted cups and saucers with pink and gilt decoration each marked in gilt 'A Present from Scarborough'. One is a moustache cup and they were clearly for sale as a pair—an early example of 'His' and 'Hers'. Height of cups 3·2″ (8·1 cm.). Diam. of saucers 6″ (15·2 cm.)

Scarborough first became a resort in the seventeenth century. In 1626 a lady walking on the sands found a spring spouting from the cliff. She tasted it and swore that it cured her maladies. The news spread. By 1667 a Dr Wittie had published his *Scarborough Spaw* extolling the virtues of the water as a 'remedy for Hypondriak, Melancolly and Windeness'. He also pointed out that salt water cured gout, establishing the superiority of a seaside spa over the inland spas. Bathing was well established as a healthful pastime by 1735 though the excessive modesty of Victorian days was yet to come.

Real development began in the 1860's. The resort was divided into two parts by the rocky promontory on which the castle stood—the north bay and the south bay. (The latter had two hydraulic lifts 'to convey passengers from the cliffs to the shore'.) In 1862 a new approach was constructed from the railway station to the harbour. The promenade pier, 1,000′ long, was built in 1869, the People's Palace and Aquarium opened in 1877 and the Spa Saloon in 1880, with a great hall to seat 1,000 people; but bathing was a major attraction. 'While some visitors are gambolling among the waves, others are riding along the sands on donkeys or horses, in order to watch the bathers and loungers.' Old photographs of late Victorian days show the men with colourful caps or strawboaters, their faces half hidden in heavy moustaches—hence the moustache cups provided with a perforated ledge inside the rim so that the liquid could be taken through a hole without wetting the moustache. What more appropriate souvenir for the period?

54a (*left*) Mug with a tinted print of 'Portobello Sands' flanked by gilded leaf sprays. Mark: MADE IN GERMANY (printed). Height 3·1″ (7·9 cm.)

54b (*right*) Pink teapot with a tinted print of 'Harbour Head, St Monan's'. Mark: MADE IN GERMANY within a circle (printed). Height 4·7″ (11·9 cm.) (Note the Harbour Head Look Out.)

Portobello did not exist at the beginning of the eighteenth century. It is said to have acquired its name when a sailor built a cottage near the shore of the Firth of Forth after returning from Admiral Edward Vernon's West Indies Expedition when he stormed Portobello in 1739. It was late in Victorian times before it became a popular watering place. *Cassell's Gazetteer* of 1900 states: 'The beach, a noble expanse of broad sand, affords safe and convenient bathing at all times of the tide, and there are warm salt-water baths. The Marine Promenade is a broad thoroughfare stretching along the sea beach, and in the centre stands the Prince of Wales Fountain. The pier has seats and a spacious saloon with pavilion above.' Golf was popular on the Portobello links at this period, which were also used as a racecourse for the Edinburgh race meetings.

St Monan's on the coast of East Fife was a small fishing port, which also accommodated 'three or four trading vessels'. The shore is of shingle and rocky ledges run out to sea. It had, however, become a small resort by the 1890's owing a great deal to its position on an attractive stretch of coast served by the East of Fife railway branch line serving Leven, Largo (birthplace of Alexander Selkirk, the original of Robinson Crusoe), Kilconquhar and Earlsferry with its golf course.

55 Pink moulded jug with an oval tinted print of 'The Pier'. Mark: MADE IN GERMANY printed in three straight lines. Height 5·2″ (13·2 cm.)

The Lincolnshire resort of Skegness developed rapidly after a railway extension of 1873 which brought many new visitors, especially from the Midlands, and the railway pressed the virtues of the town for many years. 'Skegness is so bracing,' the posters said, showing a round and robust fisherman prancing along the sand. 'The sands are firm and broad,' said the guidebooks, 'extending for miles north and south of the town.' They were the main attraction of Skegness, not only for the visitors, but for excursionists for whom there were 'donkeys, swings, coconut-shies and other amusements in full activity during the season'. In 1881 an iron promenade pier was opened with a pavilion at the end. Indeed, it was admitted that there were few other attractions in the neighbourhood. 'The surrounding country is not picturesque, but from the sand hills along the shore there are extensive views over the German Ocean and the flat marsh land reclaimed from the sea. Fine sunsets can be watched here, the sky of the Fenland being the best part of the scenery.' All the guide books of the period refer to the local 'phosphorescence'. 'During the dark nights of summer the phosphorescence of the sea is a very charming sight. At such times as one walks along the shore by the side of the receding tide, each footprint glows with phosphorescent light.'

56a (*left*) Moulded pink tobacco jar with a tinted print of the 'New Toll House to the Pier'. Unmarked (foreign). Height 4·3″ (10·9 cm.)

56b (*right*) Hotwater jug with a print of 'Southend-on-Sea from the Pier'. Printed mark: VICTORIA, AUSTRIA SCHMIDT. Height 5·9″ (14·9 cm.)

Southend-on-Sea lies on the northern side of the Thames estuary, forty miles from London. Today a large conurbation which includes Southend-on-Sea, Leigh-on-Sea, Westcliff and Thorpe Bay has a population of well over a quarter of a million people. It is interesting to trace the growth of Southend stage by stage.

1780   Southend was a village of fifty-one houses but sea bathing was already established and the first visitors had arrived.

1790   The increasing number of visitors made it necessary to build a terrace and an hotel.

1794   Facilities had to be provided for visitors who might have to face the prospect of wet days. The little resort is described as having 'an elegant library, assembly and coffee rooms'.

1801   Princess Charlotte, daughter of the Prince Regent and Caroline, Princess of Wales, was sent to Southend at the age of five to be 'immersed in salt water' for the sake of her health.

1803   Caroline, Princess of Wales, visited Southend and stayed in the terrace built in 1790, which then became the Royal Terrace. In the same year Lady Hamilton and her daughter, Horatia, visited Southend 'for sea bathing' and also stayed in the Royal Terrace, which became so popular that it could not cope with the demands for accommodation. Expansion of Southend continued. A theatre was built and 'warm' baths were provided.

1839   A wooden pier was built. However, although some visitors came by sea, most arrivals were by coach from London.

57 Three small moulded jugs, the central one with a print of 'The Pier', the others with prints of 'The Shrubbery and Beach'. All are marked '19'. Heights 3″ (7·6 cm.), 3·5″ (8·9 cm.), and 4″ (10·2 cm.) (Note: It seems from this that the manufacturers, although certainly foreign, were using inch measurements in preparing sizes for the English market. This would appear to be a 'set' of jugs.)

1845 The new Southend Railway from Liverpool Street Station to Southend (43½ miles) started to issue cheap excursion tickets.

1890– The old pier was replaced by an iron structure 1¼ miles in length, the longest pier in
  91 Britain. This had an electric tramway, was lighted by electricity and had a large pavilion near the shore end (the pier was later sold to the Great Eastern Railway). It is worth noting here that souvenir wares showing this pier must be post-1891. The dating of buildings of various kinds can be invaluable in the dating of souvenir wares. At this time the population was only 12,333.

The last decade of the nineteenth century, however, saw a phenomenal growth in the resort.

As in so many resorts which developed at this period, there was a 'select' area and a part of the town that was regarded less highly. The West Cliff with the esplanade below and the slopes from the cliff planted as a 'Shrubbery' was the fashionable part. The shops and small houses were found in the old town, east of the pier.

58*a* (*left*) Tapering mug with a tinted print of Southsea 'Clarence
Esplanade and Pier'. Mark: Crossed swords in underglaze blue.
Donath subsidiary. Height 3·5" (8·9 cm.)

58*b* (*right*) Reverse side of mug with a view of the 'Floating Bridge,
Portsmouth'.

Southsea lies within the borough of Portsmouth and occupies the south-west portion of Portsea
Island. In 1850 only two or three rough tracks crossed the wastelands now covered with streets
and houses. By the end of the century it was a flourishing resort, described in a guide book of
1897 as follows:

'It is largely favoured as a place of residence by retired or idle officers of both services, who
enjoy the stir of parades, reviews and regimental bands by land, and the view of the Solent constantly alive with yachts, steam-boats and men-of-war. It differs from the conventional bathing
place in its front being separated from sea and esplanade by the wide stretch of the Common,
which serves as an arena for so many military displays.'

At the west end of the Common is the Clarence Esplanade Pier. 'The Esplanade stretching
from this point to the fortifications of Southsea Castle, is protected by a substantial sea-wall of
brick and concrete; a carriage drive and parade run parallel with the south-eastern portion of the
wall, which is interrupted between the castle and Lumps Fort by the South Parade Pier. Steamers
from Portsmouth call at the Clarence Pier for the Isle of Wight, and at the South Parade Pier for
Sea View and Bembridge.'

Visitors to Southsea always explore Portsmouth and many cross the harbour to Gosport. In
the 1900's not only was there a steamlaunch ferry but there was also a powerful floating bridge
'available at any period of the tide, every ten minutes, for vehicles as well as passengers'.

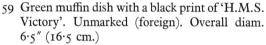

59 Green muffin dish with a black print of 'H.M.S. Victory'. Unmarked (foreign). Overall diam. 6·5″ (16·5 cm.)

60 Pink moulded ash tray with a pig smoking a gilded pipe, with a tinted print of 'South Parade Pier, Southsea'. Unmarked (foreign). Width 6″ (15·2 cm.)

Portsmouth, 'the largest royal naval establishment and strongest fortress in Britain', was of importance in the time of Henry I, a naval station in the reign of King John, and was fortified by Edward IV, Richard III and Henry VII. It subsequently became the principal station for the Royal Navy in the reign of Henry VIII.

In the 1890's H.M.S. *Victory*, on which Lord Nelson was killed at the Battle of Trafalgar (21st October 1805), was moored in the harbour and served as flagship of the Admiral of the station. It proved a great attraction for visitors. An account at this period states that 'this historic vessel has been repaired and restored until but little remains of the glorious ship that carried Nelson's flag at Trafalgar. You are still permitted to see the spot where England's great naval hero received his death-wound, and also the corner in the cockpit where his indomitable spirit passed away.'

Portsmouth Dockyard is described as follows: 'This is the largest dockyard in the kingdom (120 acres) and from its resources the most important in the world. On the east is the Royal Naval College, built in 1817; and in a line with the Mast Houses are the Hemp and Sea-Store Houses, the Rigging House with its Clock Tower and the Sail Loft. Westward lies the Docks which were greatly extended in 1876.'

H.M.S. *Victory* today lies in the dockyard—no longer afloat but still a great attraction for visitors.

61*a* (*left*) Saucer with underglaze black print of 'Birnbeck Pier'. The rim is painted with pink enamel. Unmarked (English). Height 5·5″ (14 cm.)

61*b* (*right*) Two-handled mug (c 1860) with underglaze black print of 'Weston-super-Mare' on each side. A rope motif decorates the handles and the inside of the rim. Unmarked (English). Height 4″ (10·2 cm.)

Weston-super-Mare had a population of 163 in 1811 but it had already started to develop into a watering-place with safe sea bathing on a gently shelving sandy shore. It grew rapidly when the branch line of the Bristol and Exeter Railway started to bring trippers from Bristol and elsewhere. W. R. Palmer in *A Century of Weston-super-Mare History* recalls their arrival in 1885. 'They came in crowds, often a great many more than the inhabitants of the town and, not having enough carriages, they brought them in trucks, with forms put across for seats and an awning over them, as many as thirty or forty thousand some times.'

By 1890 the town had completed the first main stage in its development. 'In 1887 a new sea front was completed, forming a continuous promenade, 2½ miles long, well provided with wind shelters and seats. The Pier, a handsome iron structure, starts from Anchor Head, the entrance being by elaborate iron gates, and continues in a straight line to the island of Birnbeck, a distance of 1,040 ft. . . . A landing stage runs out at a right angle to the pier, and in a northerly direction, whereby it is well sheltered from the prevailing westerly gales, and otherwise well adapted for the large traffic which it receives from the Welsh coast.'

62a (*left*) Cup with underglaze black print of 'The Esplanade'. The
rim has been painted with pink enamel. Unmarked (English).
Height 2·7″ (6·8 cm.)

62b (*right*) Cup (c 1905) with tinted overglaze print of the 'New Pier'.
Mark: 'Florentine China. Made in England' printed within concentric circles. Height 2·6 (6·6 cm.)

A new pier was started in 1903 with a pavilion extending from the end of Regent Street. This was
opened in 1904 and an Austrian band conducted by Herr Kant played for the occasion. There
were shops under the promenade of the Pavilion. W. R. Palmer writes: 'When it was finished I
took one of the shops, had it fitted up and opened it with toys and fancy goods. My daughter did
very well there for the first two or three seasons, then trade fell off, and I gave it up and took a
shop in the Arcade, which was then in its glory and having its best days.'

Later the pier was extended beyond the Pavilion but the added custom did not compensate for
the cost.

At the northern end of Weston Bay lies the wooded Worlebury Hill, which shelters the town
from the north winds. To the south the promontory of Brean Down juts out over a mile into the
Bristol Channel. At one time there were plans to turn this end of the bay into a major Atlantic
port and the first stone pier was started in 1864. In 1872, however, a great storm carried away the
pier and the project was abandoned. Meanwhile, the War Office had built a fort at the end of
Brean Down with seven 7″ guns. This stood intact until 1900 when a soldier, returning from
a trip to Burnham, fired a shot into one of the magazines and much of the building was destroyed.
It was on Brean Down in 1897 that Marconi carried out one of the earliest experiments in wire-
less telegraphy, when signals were successfully transmitted across the nine-mile stretch of the
Bristol Channel to Lavernock in South Wales.

63a (*left*) Pierced moulded plate with tinted print of 'The Esplanade' enclosed in a gilded circle. Mark: A shield with a lion and the words 'Schumann' and 'Bavaria' above and below respectively. Diam. 8·5″ (21·7 cm.)

63b (right) A similar plate with a view of 'Weymouth from the Nothe'.

The watering place now known as Weymouth was at one time known as Melcombe Regis. Weymouth proper straggled 'over low hills with winding streets and alleys on the west side of the Wey'. Today they form a single town.

The bay with its sandy beach became a fashionable bathing place towards the end of the eighteenth century when George III made frequent visits, staying at Gloucester House, now a hotel. An equestrian statue of the monarch was erected by the townspeople in 1809 to commemorate the fiftieth anniversary of his accession. The town has many fine Georgian buildings.

Weymouth became the Great Western Railway packet station for the Channel Islands. 'The harbour is protected on the south-east by a concrete breakwater extending from the Nothe fort; a pier forms the entrance to the north side of the harbour, and the Nothe forms the south-west side . . . The Esplanade is a handsome terrace fronting the sea, about a mile in length and provided with sheltered seats.' (*Cassell's Gazetteer* for 1900).

Photographs taken in late Victorian times show not only innumerable individual bathing machines on the sands but also larger structures on wheels standing in the water, each divided into cubicles. These were approached by narrow portable wooden jetties.

64a (*centre*) Pierced plate with pale brown decoration and an overglaze tinted print of 'Ryde from Ryde Pier'. Unmarked (foreign). Diam. 9″ (22·9 cm.)

64b (*right and left*) Pair of moulded gilded shoes printed in gilt with 'A Present from Yarmouth, Isle of Wight'. Unmarked (foreign). Length of each shoe 6″ (15·2 cm.)

An account of 1895 tells us that 'Ryde is practically the chief town of the Isle of Wight, and the centre of the summer season, as well as a very favourite place of residence—a distinction it owes in part to its position as the most frequented landing place, the crossing here occupying less than half an hour . . . '. Ryde dates the beginning of its prosperity from the construction of its pier, which was commenced by a joint-stock company in 1813, and opened the following year, its length then being 1,740 ft. The pierhead and pavilion date from 1842, and many other improvements have been made. The present length of the pier is about 2,280 ft. and its extremity commands a view of Spithead, Portsmouth, Calshot Castle and Southampton Water.

Yarmouth, on the western side of the island, is also a 'landing place' to which the steamers sailed from Lymington. 'The carriers, which take passengers, leave Yarmouth in the morning for the capital of the island'.

Many souvenirs of other places in the Isle of Wight may readily be collected—Newport, Sandown, Shanklin, Carisbrooke Castle, Cowes, Osborne House and, of course, those little glass lighthouses filled with the coloured sands of Alum Bay, though these, like the Yarmouth shoes shown above, are not 'pictorial' souvenirs.

65*a* (*left*) Pink moulded teapot printed overglaze with a view of 'The Beach' encircled in gilt. Unmarked (foreign). Height 4″ (10·2 cm.)

65*b* (*right*) Moulded teapot with gilded decoration and an overglaze black print of a 'View from the Pier'. Unmarked (foreign). Height 5·2″ (13·2 cm.)

Worthing first gained popularity when Amelia, youngest child of George III, visited the town in the first decade of the nineteenth century. It developed more slowly than Brighton and was a quieter resort. Protected by an amphitheatre of hills, it gained a reputation for its mild climate 'well adapted for delicate persons in winter'. Many people came as visitors and decided to live in the town in later life. A pier and esplanade were built and in 1889 the pier was extended.

Unfortunately, Worthing's drainage was not above reproach. In 1892 and 1893 there were serious outbreaks of typhoid fever and as a result there was a thorough overhaul of the whole system after which development continued.

The shore at Worthing consists of a shingle beach above a broad stretch of sand, and wooden groynes were constructed to prevent the drift of shingle. The shingle did not, however, prevent bathing. It was possible to run the bathing machines into the water where there was a sandy bottom.

Descriptive writers of the 1890's refer to the prevalence of seaweed on the beach 'which accumulates in such quantities as to become a perfect nuisance'. Today's concern is mainly over the possibility of oil pollution, which so often threatens the south coast resorts.

5 The Tourist Centres

There were many places besides the Spas and the seaside resorts which attracted visitors and of these the greatest tourist attraction of all was London, the capital City of a great Empire and a magnet which attracted visitors from throughout the world. It would not be difficult to build up a sizeable collection of London items alone and one may expect to see all the well known sights pictured in many different forms, such as the gilded chocolate service shown in Plate No. 130. An odd omission is the lack of souvenirs of Buckingham Palace, until it is remembered that Queen Victoria during her long years of widowhood hardly ever used it, so that it lacked the magic attraction of Royalty that it has today.

The London street scenes are most rewarding. Not only has the horse traffic disappeared but, regrettably perhaps, so have some of the buildings. Against the background of pictorial souvenirs of London Bridge it was most interesting to follow the dismantling of the Bridge and the completion of a new one; whilst a short distance away the Royal Exchange remains unchanged against a dramatically altered background of the new Stock Exchange, to say nothing of the rebuilt Bank of England. We can also see the first souvenirs showing the 'New Tower Bridge' which, whilst still a bridge, is no longer required to cope with the shipping traffic which has disappeared. The outstanding building of them all, the Tower of London, was difficult to portray because of its size and shape, and it is St Paul's Cathedral, miraculously spared by all the bombs of the last War, that has been commemorated most frequently from earliest times. Westminster Abbey on the other hand, like the Tower of London, was not easy to illustrate and there are few souvenirs.

The other big cities all had their souvenirs, but most had grown prodigiously with the Industrial Revolution and had few historic places of interest to commemorate. The University towns of Oxford and Cambridge, on the other hand, must have provided a sizeable market for souvenirs for many generations; however, we have found not a single continental piece relating to them, which is not to say that there were not any. We expect to find the old traditional centres for tourists well represented, that is castles, abbeys and monastic ruins, Stratford-on-Avon, Stonehenge, etc., and indeed they are. Included among them must be the Royal Palaces—Windsor, Osborne House (I.O.W.), Balmoral and Sandringham, but, as mentioned above, nothing is so far recorded for Buckingham Palace. Osborne House was not strictly speaking a Palace but the private residence of Queen Victoria, built to the ideas of Prince Albert, but many souvenirs of this House were produced.

Although none of the Fairs themselves were commemorated by souvenirs, the enormous number of small, out of the way places which have been illustrated must be of great interest to any local collector and there are some charming small pieces, of which we can show only a few. We have however included some examples of folk ware, which are illustrated, but not with named views, and could well have been sold as Fairings suitable to the locality.

66a (*left*) Moulded pottery child's plate with black underglaze print of the Thames Tunnel. Below the scene are the words: '1200 ft. long, 76 ft. below high water mark, was 8 years building and cost £446,000. Opened the 25th day March 1843.' Unmarked (English). Diam. 7·3″ (18·5 cm.)

66b (*right*) Plate with a black underglaze print of 'The Crystal Palace 1851' and the words 'A Present from London'. Gilded rim. Unmarked (English). Diam. 6·1″ (15·5 cm.)

Many souvenirs were made to mark important events. The above are typical examples and both are dated. The Thames Tunnel was projected by Sir Mark Isambard Brunel and was begun in 1825. Flooding suspended work for some years and it was not completed until 1843, linking Wapping and Rotherhithe. Annual fairs were held in the tunnel. In 1853 the fair was brilliantly illuminated and attracted 40,000 people. In 1865 the tunnel was purchased by the East London Railway Company which opened its line for traffic in 1876. The tunnel is still used by London Transport.

The building of the Crystal Palace for the Great Exhibition of 1851 brought a flood of souvenirs, which is not surprising since it attracted some six million visitors in twenty-four weeks, and excursion trains were run to London from many parts of the country. The design was by Sir Joseph Paxton. The building was of prefabricated iron and glass and covered nineteen acres in Hyde Park. The Exhibition itself was sponsored by the Prince Consort to unite 'the industry and art of all the nations of the earth'. A prize-winning essay on the purposes of the Exhibition stressed the significance of the Exhibition 'in advancing national taste by bringing in close contiguity the various productions of nearly all the nations of the earth in any way distinguished for ornamental manufacturers'.

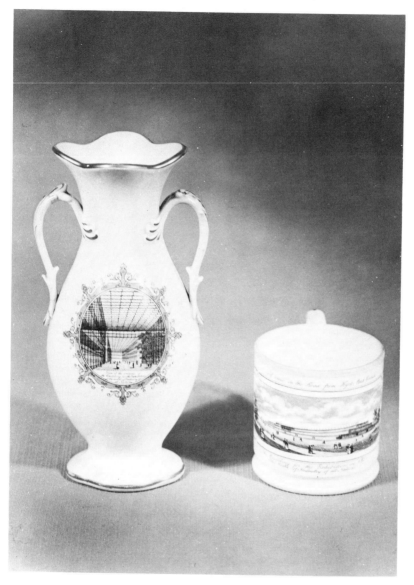

67a (left) Vase with overglaze sepia print of 'A View on the Road from Hyde Park Corner' showing 'The Buildings for the Exhibition in 1851. The works of industry of all Nations.' Framed in turquoise enamel. Rim, handles and base gilded. Mark: GREEN, LONDON 75883 with registration mark for 1851. Height 8·7″ (22·1 cm.)

67b (right) Mug with similar print. Rim and handle gilded. Mark as above. Height 3·4″ (8·6 cm.)

68 (*left to right*) Jug, teapot and mug each with a black underglaze print
of the 1862 Exhibition. All are gilded and unmarked (English).
Heights: jug 3·8″ (9·7 cm.), teapot 7·5″ (19 cm.), mug 3·2″ (8·1 cm.)

The Crystal Palace, built for the 1851 Exhibition, should not be confused with the International
Exhibition building of 1862 which was designed by Captain Fowke and stood where the Natural
History Museum now stands in the Cromwell Road. The Queen was mourning the death of Prince
Albert, who had died in 1861, so there was no Royal opening. Nevertheless, it was an occasion for
the issue of souvenirs to commemorate the event.

69 Gilded ribbon plate with black overglaze print of the Crystal Palace
and the words, 'A Present from London'. Unmarked (attributed to
Schumann). Diam. 8·5″ (21·6 cm.)

After the Great Exhibition of 1851 the Crystal Palace, which had never been intended as a permanent building, was due to be demolished. However, there was considerable pressure from the public to retain the building and it was decided to transfer it to another part of London. The chosen site was at Sydenham, in the Metropolitan Borough of Lewisham, where it was re-erected by a private company between 1852 and 1854 and opened by Queen Victoria. The building was adapted to its new site by adding transepts on the north and south sides, and in 1856 two towers were built, each 282′ high. If there is ever any doubt whether a print is of the original Crystal Palace or the Sydenham adaptation, the towers will settle the matter.

In 1911 a Festival of Empire was held in the 200-acre grounds of the Palace and when war was declared in 1914 it became a training ground for Royal Naval Volunteers. In 1920 it became the property of the nation. It became a great centre for entertainment—football matches, dog shows, brass band concerts, dirt track racing, cinema shows and many other amusements. Then in 1936 it was destroyed by fire. What would have happened to it if it had still been standing when the Second World War broke out is rather a speculation. It is unlikely to have survived, for the reflective glass would have provided a landmark for enemy aircraft.

70a (*left*) Ribbon plate decorated in grey and gilt with a tinted over-glaze print of the 'Gigantic Wheel at Earl's Court' and 'A Present from Earl's Court'. Unmarked (foreign). Diam. 6″ (15·2 cm.)

70b (*right*) Blue jug with tinted underglaze print of 'Earls Court, The Great Wheel'. Unmarked (foreign). Height 3·7″ (9·4 cm.)

The Underground station at Earl's Court, opened in 1871, provided a focal point for routes from Ealing, Richmond and Wimbledon, and was on the Inner Circle. Other lines were opened in the next ten years and Earl's Court proved to be a suitable centre for exhibitions. The first to be held was the America Exhibition of 1887, and many followed. A major attraction was the Great Wheel, which was constructed in 1894, copying a similar wheel at the World's Fair in Chicago. It took passengers on a twenty-minute trip, but the wheel stuck once and a number of people were forced to spend the night in the open 'buckets', for which each passenger received £5 in compensation. The wheel was dismantled in 1907.

The above souvenirs, although unmarked, can therefore be dated to the period 1887–1907.

71a (*left*) Pink cup with a tinted overglaze print of the Houses of
Parliament within a gilt circle. Mark: 'Made in Germany' within
concentric circles printed in brown. Height 2·8" (7·1 cm.)

71b (*right*) Teapot with tinted overglaze print of 'Fleet Street and St.
Paul's. Gilt decoration. Mark: 'Made in Germany' within concentric circles printed in brown. Height 5" (12·7 cm.)

The Old Royal Palace of Westminster was destroyed by fire in 1834, and it was necessary to build a new home for Parliament. Sir Charles Barry, R.A., designed an impressive structure in the late Gothic style and this was started in 1840, though the first Parliament did not officially assemble in the building until 1854. The most famous feature—the Clock Tower which houses Big Ben—was not completed until 1857. Work continued on the buildings until 1888. Unfortunately the material used was a magnesium limestone, which did not stand up very well to the corrosive atmosphere of London, and repair work is constantly necessary.

St Paul's Cathedral is the second building on its site. The old city church was destroyed by the Great Fire in 1666. It was rebuilt between 1675 and 1710 to a design by Sir Christopher Wren, and is regarded as his masterpiece. The building is dominated by its vast dome, which rises 365' above the floor of the church, and can be seen as a landmark from many parts of London, though skyscraper blocks now obscure some of the former views.

St Paul's Cathedral is approached from the west by way of Fleet Street, Ludgate Circus and Ludgate Hill. Fleet Street has changed a good deal over the years—the main reconstruction took place between 1897 and 1916. A new building line was defined on the south side in order to provide a street 60' wide to take the increasing traffic.

72 Pink jug with a circular print of 'The People's Palace, London' within a gilded circle. Mark: 'Made in Germany' with concentric circles printed in brown. Height 5·2″ (13 cm.)

The People's Palace was opened by Queen Victoria in 1887 as a centre for education and recreation. It included a hall devoted to exhibitions and concerts and the East London College. On 25th February 1931, the hall was destroyed by fire. It was a massive conflagration and it took 250 firemen with 55 engines, 30 tenders and 8 water towers over two hours to control the flames.

73 'Tin' plate with coloured print of Trafalgar Square showing horse-
drawn buses carrying advertisements for Bovril, Hudson's Soap and
the Alhambra. Note the 'knifeboard' buses on the right, the Hansom
cab or 'growler' and the man with the sandwich board. Diam. 10·1″
(25·6 cm.)

Trafalgar Square was designed between 1829 and 1841 as a large open space adorned with foun-
tains, statues and a column to Nelson erected between 1841 and 1843. The column was designed
by William Railton and is 176′ high, surmounted by a statue of Nelson 17′ high by E. H. Baily,
R.A. The square pedestal represents Nelson's four great battles and the huge lions at the corners,
designed by Sir Edwin Landseer, were added in 1868.

74a (*left*) Pierced plate moulded with oak leaves and acorns with a tinted overglaze print of the 'Royal Exchange'. Mark: 'Made in Germany' in a circle printed overglaze (probably Unger & Schilde of Saxony). Diam. 8·2″ (20·8 cm.)

74b (*right*) Fluted plate with a pink border and a tinted overglaze print of 'The City with Royal Exchange'. Mark: 'Made in Germany' with concentric circles. Diam. 8·1″ (20·6 cm.)

The Royal Exchange was built on the site of two previous Exchange buildings, both destroyed by fire, from designs by William Tite. There are eight Corinthian columns on the facade, each 41′ high. It was opened in 1844 by Queen Victoria, accompanied by the Prince Consort. The Duke of Wellington was also present, for in front of the building had been placed an equestrian statue of the Duke executed by Sir Francis Legatt Chantry, who had died three years previously. In 1920, after the First World War, a war memorial of Portland stone in the form of a pillar surmounted by a lion was designed by Sir Aston Webb, R.A., and placed in front of the Exchange. The horse-drawn omnibus ran to the City in 1837. In 1851 the 'knifeboard' bus—the first to carry passengers—was introduced. Hansom cabs or 'growlers' appeared in the 1850's and throughout Victorian times there was a jostle of wagons, carriages and donkey carts in all the busy streets. Bicycles appeared before the end of the century, followed by motor cars, though not before the Locomotive Act of 1865 was repealed in 1896, making it unnecessary for a boy with a red flag to precede every vehicle.

The Royal Exchange has been occupied by the Royal Exchange Assurance Company since it was founded in 1720.

75 Enlarged print of 'London Bridge' from plate with pale pink border.
Mark: MADE IN BOHEMIA printed in a circle. Diam. 9·4″
(23·4 cm.)

A London Bridge goes back to the very origins of London and there have been four since 1066.
Now there is a fifth, opened in March 1973 by H.M. the Queen. The one that has just disappeared
was built by John Rennie and his sons between 1824 and 1831 of Scottish and Devonshire granite.
The old bridge pictured above was demolished and has now been re-erected in Havusa City,
Arizona—a tourist centre with London buses—and from the stone of the old bridge souvenirs
have been made over which, purchasers are told, 'all the crown heads of Europe and notability
have passed at one time or another since the bridge was built'. With this unique history, souvenirs
of the bridge will always be sought after.

76a (*left*) Grey-blue moulded and indented plate (c 1894) with a central overglaze black print of 'New Tower Bridge' within a gilded circle. Unmarked (Foreign). Diam. 7·8″ (19·8 cm.)

76b (*right*) Indented moulded plate with an overglaze black print of 'The Tower' and the words 'A Present from London'. Unmarked (Foreign). Diam. 8·7″ (22·1 cm.)

When the Tower Bridge was built it provided communication across the Thames which had been urgently needed at this point for many years. The necessary Act was passed in 1885; the foundation stone was laid by the Prince of Wales in 1886 and the work was completed by 1894 to a design by Sir John Wolfe Barry and Sir Horace Jones. Souvenirs of the completed bridge were therefore made after this date. The construction is such that the low-level passage is on the 'bascule' principle—the centre span of 200′ is divided in two, each half being pivoted and furnished with a counterpoise, and hauled upward and back against the Gothic towers when the waterway is opened. A high level footway (now closed) was provided from tower to tower, access being afforded by lifts. The side spans are on the suspension principle.

For hundreds of years the Tower itself was the centre of feudal history, and the background of its darkest scenes. It started as a palace and then became a prison and place of execution. Finally it became an armoury and museum, in which are kept the Crown Jewels. The Norman Keep, or White Tower, is in the Inner Ward which is surrounded by a massive wall with thirteen towers. Then comes the Outer Ward, surrounded by a second wall with eight towers, six facing the river. Little construction work has been done since the eighteenth century so that the building itself will not reveal the date of a particular souvenir; one has to depend on external features with landscape or a ceramic mark if there is one.

77
Square bowl (1830) with indented corners and an underglaze
blue print of 'Vauxhall Gardens'.
The border is a continuous
band of ivy leaves. Unmarked
(English). Width 9·2″ (24·3
cm.). Height 3·3″ (8·4 cm.)

The famous Vauxhall (Fox Hall) Pleasure Gardens were sited behind the present Albert Embank-
ment, close to Vauxhall Bridge. From about 1661, when they were known as the New Spring
Gardens, until the summer of 1859, they attracted several thousand London pleasure-seekers
every summer evening. They opened at 5.00 p.m. and after dusk the gardens were illuminated.
Opposite the entrance was a Gothic rotunda where the band played and small pavilions provided
suppers and wines.

At first the Vauxhall Gardens attracted a fashionable clientele and they reached the peak of their
popularity in the eighteenth century. In the nineteenth century they were less fashionable and
gradually became a resort of the middle and lower classes.

In 1845 many balloon ascents were made from the grounds, but these were the last excitements.
In 1859 Vauxhall Gardens were sold by auction and, as such, ceased to exist.

The dish shown above is of special interest. Whether such bowls were sold singly as souvenirs,
or not, we shall probably never know, for large dinner services of blue and white transfer ware,
which often included bowls, frequently carried prints of places. Some services carried pictures of
Blackfriars Bridge, the Mansion House and St Paul's Cathedral, for example.

Aston Hall is a fine example of the Jacobean style. Here Charles I was entertained for two days prior to the Battle of Edgehill. The property was acquired by the Corporation of Birmingham and thrown open as a public park in 1684. The Hall is now furnished by the City Art Gallery with pictures and furniture of the period.

78a Earthenware mug with green under-
78b glaze print of Aston Hall and the Town Hall, Birmingham. The rim is decorated with entwined vine branches. Unmarked (English). Diam. 5″ (12·7 cm.)

The Town Hall, Birmingham was completed in 1850. All four sides are adorned with massive detached columns copied from those of the Temple of Jupiter Stator, Rome, the whole fabric resting on an arcaded basement 23 ft. high.

79 Moulded plate with overglaze tinted print of the 'Suspension
Bridge, Clifton' enclosed in a wide blue-green decorative band with
gilding. Unmarked (foreign). Diam. 9″ (22·9 cm.)

The Clifton Suspension Bridge spans the Avon Gorge at Bristol. A sum was left in the eighteenth
century for a bridge and one was designed by Isambard Kingdom Brunel in 1831. Abutments
were made, but the work stopped in 1843 and was not resumed until 1861. The bridge is 702 ft.
long and 245 ft. above high water. Thus, three-masted ships were able to pass beneath.

80a (*left*) Pottery plate with an underglaze tinted print of 'Netherport and French Ambassador's House' and 'Souvenir of Old Edinborough'. Unmarked. Diam. 9·1″ (23·1 cm.)

80b (*right*) Kettle (c 1890–1900) with an overglaze tinted print of 'The Forth Bridge'. Mark: 'Made in Germany' within concentric circles. Height 4·5″ (11·4 cm.)

The Netherport, or Nether Bow Port as it is more usually called, was a defensive gateway which once divided the burgh of Edinburgh from the ecclesiastical burgh of Canongate. It was situated at the end of the High Street close to John Knox's House at the corner of Jeffrey Street and St Mary's Street. The Nether Bow Port was associated with the 'Forty Five' rebellion. When the Prince marched on Edinburgh, he sent a man in lowland dress to call at the gate and ask to enter. But the guards were suspicious. However, a coach and horses clattered down the road to leave the city and when the gates were opened to let it pass the Highlanders rushed in, overpowered the guard, and the Prince's army gained entrance. The French Ambassador's House was two buildings down on the left going towards Holyrood.

The Forth Bridge is an obvious subject for a souvenir. This steel viaduct took six years to complete and, when it was opened by the Prince of Wales in 1890, was the largest bridge in the world. It is partly supported on symmetrical and slender-looking pillars of granite, and partly rises from sunk concrete foundations under water and from the island of Inchgarvie, in the form of girders on the cantilever or bracket system. The bridge measures 1½ miles in length, of which 1 mile is spanned by cantilevers, the main spans being each of 1,700′, and the pinnacle of the structure is 450′ above the water. The largest vessels can pass under the arches.

81a (*left*) Tapering pint mug (c 1894) with black underglaze prints
'The Manchester Ship Canal' and a portrait of 'Daniel Adamson'.
Rope motif on rim and handle. Mark: Patented 31st March 1882 by
J. Tams, Longton, Staffs on a ribbon. Height 4·6″ (11·7 cm.)

81b (*right*) Fluted plate (1887) with black underglaze print of views of
the 'Exchange', 'Town Hall' and 'Infirmary', Manchester and of
the 'Royal Jubilee Exhibition' Manchester 1887. Above is a portrait of Queen Victoria and on either side of the portrait seascapes
with the captions 'Jamaica to Manchester' and 'Manchester to New
York £4·10'. Mark: Franz Ant. Mehlem Bonn A Rhein impressed
in a circle. Diam. 9·8″ (22·6 cm.)

The building of the Manchester Ship Canal began in 1887, the first sod being cut at Eastham
Ferry, on the Cheshire side of the Mersey. The filling of the canal commenced in 1893 and it was
formally opened on New Year's Day 1894. Five million pounds were lent for the project by the
Corporation of Manchester in consideration of majority power on the Board. The souvenir mug
was probably made for the opening occasion. The date it carries refers to an earlier patent
described in the Pottery Gazette of 1886 as 'the newest and best Government Stamped Earthenware Measure in the market'.

The Manchester Royal Jubilee Exhibition plate reflects civic pride and the rapid development
of the city. The Royal Infirmary had been completed in 1853, the Royal Exchange in 1869, and
the Gothic Town Hall from designs by Alfred Waterhouse in 1877. It is ironic, in view of this
proud record, that the plate chosen as a souvenir for the Exhibition should have been made by
the German pottery of Franz A. Mehlem at Bonn, rather than in one of the nearby Staffordshire
potteries. It is particularly interesting since most of the German souvenirs are of porcelain. No
other example of souvenir pottery from Germany has so far been recorded.

NOTTINGHAM CASTLE & PARK

82*a* (*left*) Octagonal earthenware plate with gilded rim and sprays of flowers and with underglaze coloured transfer print of Nottingham market square. Printed mark: A beehive between two floral sprays with Trade Mark on a panel below which is printed Wallis Gimson & Co. Diam. 8·5″ (21·8 cm.)

82*b* (*right*) A similar plate with an enlarged view of 'Nottingham Castle & Park' showing the ruins of the Castle with no roof or windows. A man is mowing the lawn in front of the scaffolding of a grandstand.

The Corn Exchange, as it was called, was pulled down and the large open air market moved between the Wars to make way for the present City Hall. The market square was the site of the famous Michaelmas Goose Fair, which disrupted the centre of the City for a week until it was also moved when the open air market closed.

Nottingham Castle was built by William the Conqueror. It was a huge fortress and one of his first, but after a glamorous history was demolished by Cromwell in 1651. The first Duke of Newcastle then erected a residence in the classical style, 1674–9, which was gutted by the mob in the Reform Riots of 1831 and remained the ruin seen in the picture for over forty years. The then Duke sued the Citizens of Nottingham for the damages and obtained an award of £22,000 in 1842. A model of the ruins was made and used as an exhibit in the case, and is now displayed. The building was then restored and opened in 1878 as the first Provincial Museum of the Fine and Decorative Arts by the Prince and Princess of Wales. What is curious is that the makers of this plate, Wallis Gimson & Co., only traded under this title from 1884–90 but were using an obsolete picture hardly likely to appeal to anyone with knowledge of the Castle's proud new role.

The presence of a lawn mower is interesting. It may not be generally known that the original machine was invented by Edwin Budding as far back as 1830. He was a manufacturer of machines for shearing cloth and conceived the idea that the same principle could be used for shearing the grass. Messrs Ransomes acquired the manufacturing rights and made the first mower in 1832, and have continued to produce them ever since. Mr Budding said of the machine, 'Country gentlemen will find in using my machine an amusing and healthful exercise'. Present day users may wonder where the amusing part came in.

83a (*left*) Two-handled pottery mug with underglaze black print of 'Corfe Castle'. Dealer's mark: J. Spicer, 67 High West Street, Dorchester. Height 4·7″ (11·9 cm.)

83b (*right*) Heavy porcelain plate (c 1890) with overglaze black print of 'Cardiff Castle'. Impressed mark: 'WORCESTER' below a crown. Diam. 7·8″ (19·8 cm.)

Corfe Castle in Dorset was an ancient borough by prescription and was incorporated in the reign of Queen Elizabeth, who granted it the same privileges as those belonging to the Cinque Ports. The actual Castle which gives the village its name was built in the tenth century on a crest of the Purbeck Hills. Today it is a ruin after destruction by the Parliamentary troops in 1646. It is interesting to note that Corfe Castle souvenirs were marketed through a dealer in the old market town of Dorchester.

Cardiff Castle dates from the eleventh century and in it Robert, Duke of Normandy, brother of Henry I, died after a confinement of twenty-eight years. In the Civil War, after three days' bombardment, it was treacherously delivered to Cromwell, who immediately hanged the traitor. A gazetteer of 1900 states: 'Cardiff Castle is partly ruinous, the habitable portion being the seat of the Marquis of Bute.'

84a (*left*) Tapering mug with a black underglaze print of 'Romsey Abbey Church, Hants'. Unmarked (English). Diam. 2·9″ (7·4 cm.)

84b (*centre*) Plate with overglaze black print of 'Tewkesbury Abbey'. Unmarked (English). Diam. 6·2″ (15·7 cm.)

84c (*right*) Mug with overglaze print of Malmesbury Abbey. Unmarked. (English). Height 3″ (7·6 cm.)

The building of the Abbey Church of Saints Mary and Ethelflaeda at Romsey began in the reign of Henry I as part of a Benedictine nunnery and includes some of the finest Norman work in the country. In 1539 the nunnery was dissolved and the parishioners were able to buy the building for £100. A major restoration took place in 1892 and further work has been carried out recently. The view on the mug appears to have been made prior to the restoration of 1892.

The Abbey Church at Tewkesbury was part of a Benedictine monastery of the twelfth century. Much was rebuilt in the fourteenth century but the central tower is probably original. When the Abbey was surrendered in 1539 there were thirty-eight monks. Most of the Abbey buildings were destroyed, but the church was purchased by the parishioners. It was restored between 1874 and 1879.

Malmesbury takes its name from Maldulph, who established a hermitage and a school in the seventh century at which the celebrated Aldhelm, Bishop of Sherborne, was educated. Aldhelm was for a time Abbot of Malmesbury and founded a Benedictine Abbey of which only parts remain. The present Abbey church, which became the parish church, incorporates the parts of the original abbey church which were saved after the Reformation. These include some fine carved figures of the apostles in the walls of the porch.

85a (*left*) Tapering mug with black band decoration and a sepia print of 'Jervaulx Abbey, Wensleydale'. Dealer's mark: James Autun, China Rooms, Leyburn. (English.) Height 3·2″ (8·1 cm.)

85b (*centre*) Porcelain double-handled mug with underglaze black print of Wells Cathedral 'West' on one side 'East' on the other. Dealer's mark: Herring, Wells (English). Height 4″ (10·2 cm.)

85c (*right*) Porcelain spill vase with an overglaze black print of 'Bruton Church, Somerset'. (English.) Dealer's mark: T. Autcliffe, China Rooms, Bruton, on a ribbon band. Height 3·7″ (9·4 cm.)

The buildings shown on the three pictorial souvenirs above are all fine examples of their kind. Bruton Church is a magnificent specimen of Perpendicular architecture. Wells Cathedral has always attracted visitors, and so has Jervaulx Abbey, the ruined Cistercian Monastery in Wensleydale (note that the souvenir for the latter was sponsored by a dealer in Leyburn, five miles distant). Local markets must have provided opportunities for selling such souvenirs even in the case of Wells. The Market House in Wells, built in 1835, is adjacent to the Cathedral and had a market every Saturday. Fairs were held in January, May, November and December. At Priddy on the Mendips, not far from Wells, the annual sheep fair is still held every August.

Note that all three mugs carry the marks of local dealers who must have ordered them in sufficient numbers to justify the service.

86 Moulded plates with gilded oakleaf-and-acorn decoration and tinted
overglaze prints of:
  (*left*) Winchester Cathedral, West Front.
  (*right*) St Cross Hospital, Winchester.
Marks: (*left*) 'Made in Germany' printed in brown within concen-
    tric circles. Within the circle 'for C. R. Payne, Winchester.'
    (*right*) 'Manufactured in Germany' printed in a straight
    line in black. Diam. 5·5″ (14 cm.)
The footrims of these plates are bored to take a wire or cord for
hanging. These plates must be attributed to the same maker.

Winchester lies only twelve miles from Southampton and has always been a tourist centre. More-
over, even as late as 1900, it had many markets and fairs at which souvenirs could be sold by an
enterprising local dealer. 'Markets are held on Wednesday and Saturday . . . the fairs are held on
the first Monday in Lent and on October 23 and 24, St. Magdalen's on August 2, and St. Giles
on September 12 for cheese.' The Cathedral dates from the eleventh century and 'stands in a
spacious close crossed by a magnificent avenue of elms and lime trees leading up to the west
front, the finest in England of those that have no towers.'

The Hospital of St Cross was founded in 1136 by Henry de Blois, Bishop of Winchester, for
poor men described in the Charter of 1185 as 'poor impotent men, reduced in strength as rarely
to be able to support themselves without the assistance of another', and these were provided with
'garments and beds suitable to their infirmities'. These former functions are no longer needed,
but visitors who come to see the Church of St Cross have always been made aware of its origins.
'To the left of Beaufort's gatehouse is the porter's lodge, where a horn of beer and a manchet of
bread are offered to every visitor.'

Today there are two orders of Brethren of St Cross. The black gown worn by the Knights
Hospitalers distinguishes them from the Brethren of the Beaufort (extension of noble poverty),
who wear the dark red cloak of Beaufort. The well-known tradition of a 'Wayfarer's Dole' remains
today.

87 Hexagonal moulded earthenware tray (c 1825–35) by T. & J. Carey, with an underglaze black print of York Cathedral. Printed shield-shaped mark with the words 'York Cathedral' surmounted by a mitre. Width, including handles 15″ (38·1 cm.)

The present building of York Minster was completed in 1472. In 1829 the choir was set on fire by a fanatic and there was another serious fire in 1840. Since then there has been much restoration, which continues today. The view above shows the West Front, said to be 'more architecturally perfect than any other English Cathedral'. That was a view expressed in Victorian times.

The makers of this tray (some would call it a tureen stand, which it may well have been) were T. and J. Carey. This particular example has been hung on a wall as decoration for many years and such pieces, whatever their original use, may reasonably be regarded as reminders of the places they illustrate.

88*a* (*left*) Tapering mug with overglaze black print of 'Charterhouse School, Godalming'. Mark: 'Made in Germany' between concentric circles, printed in brown. Height 3·4″ (8·6 cm.)

88*b* (*right*) Mug with overglaze black print of 'Trinity College, Cambridge', showing the Great Court. Unmarked (English). Height 3·4″ (8·6 cm.)

Collectors will sometimes find souvenir pieces with a view of a school or college. No doubt these were sold in the town to pupils, students and their relatives, either to keep as souvenirs or to give away as presents. They are by no means common but would make a most interesting collection.

Charterhouse School moved from London to Godalming in 1872. The main buildings exhibit a combination of early English and decorated Gothic features and enclose a square which is entered through a gatehouse tower of 130′. Most views of Charterhouse are taken from the cricket field.

Trinity College, Cambridge, owes the Great Court shown on the souvenir mug to the imagination of Thomas Nevile, who became Master of Trinity in 1593. Its main features are the Clock Tower and the fountain, built in 1602. Until the nineteenth century this provided the main supply of water for the college.

89a (*left*) Similar plaque with a view of Chester Cathedral with pattern no. 3356. Both plates measure 9·8″ (24·9 cm). in diam.

89b (*right*) Decorative plaque moulded in relief in a form of hard plaster with a view of Eaton Hall (tinted). The rim is pierced for hanging. Mark: 'Made in Austria' 3357.

Eaton Hall, known to hundreds of young men who went through the Officers' Cadet Training Unit there during and after the last War, was situated four miles south of Chester, and was built in 1866 in florid Gothic style as the seat of the Duke of Westminster. It has now been demolished.

Chester Cathedral was originally the church of St Werburgh, established in 1053. The present building, which is of red sandstone, exhibits work in every style from Norman to late Perpendicular. The general restoration of the cathedral, begun in 1868, was carried out under the supervision of Sir Gilbert Scott.

Abbotsford was the mansion and seat of Sir Walter Scott (1771-1832) on the right bank of the Tweed in the Parish of Melrose, a property which he purchased in 1812. In architecture the mansion defies all rules, and many of its details are copies of old and widely-differing features from various buildings. Its main interest is in the associations, and especially the study which Scott was able to approach from his bedroom unobserved. Here he did much of his writing. He worked with great energy and his output was prodigious.

90 Plate with black underglaze print of 'Abbotsford, Selkirkshire' marked in script with this title on the base. (English) Diam. 6·5″ (16·5 cm.)

91 Decorative plaque moulded in relief to form a view of the 'Castle and Flora Macdonald Statue, Inverness'. Mark: 2542 AUSTRIA

Inverness Castle was built in 1834 on the site of earlier buildings. It is of red sandstone, castellated in the Tudor style, and today it houses the County Police Offices and the Courts of Justice.

The esplanade in front of the south porch has a memorial to Flora Macdonald by the local sculptor, Andrew Davidson.

Flora Macdonald was the heroine of the Jacobite Rebellion who made it possible for Prince Charles to escape from the Hebrides.

92 Engraving from Camden's *Britannia* (1695 edition).

The large group of standing stones on Salisbury Plain in Wiltshire have always attracted sight-seers who have wondered and speculated about their origin. The engraving (Plate No. 92) from Camden's *Britannia* shows them as visitors saw them at the end of the seventeenth century. Camden gave as his opinion that the stones were 'not natural but artificial, being made of fine sand cemented together with a glewy sort of matter'. The plate made for the tourist trade in the nineteenth century shows the stones before the Ministry of Works carried out the 'restoration' some years ago, and the photograph shows the stones as they are today.

96

93 Plate with black underglaze print of 'Stonehenge, Wilts'. Dealer's mark: Watson, Salisbury. Unmarked (English). Diam. 5·4″ (13·7 cm.)

94 Stonehenge today.

95a (*left*) Fluted cup and saucer with underglaze black print of the 'High Street, Haslemere'. Unmarked (foreign). Height of cup 2·5" (6·3 cm.)

95b (*right*) Teapot with gilding and rectangular overglaze print of the 'High Street, Haslemere, Surrey'. Mark: 'Made in Germany' printed in black within concentric circles. Height 5·3" (13·5 cm.)

The cup and saucer are part of a tea set and the teapot was made by a different manufacturer, indicating that there must have been a market for more than the odd souvenir.

Haslemere was a well known beauty spot and in the latter part of last century started to attract residents devoted to culture, so much so that the town's motto became 'Vita Musis Gratior'—'life is more satisfying through the arts'. Lord Tennyson, George Eliot and Conan Doyle all lived in the neighbourhood; the Dolmetsch family, the world famous early-music revivalists and instrument makers, have also made Haslemere famous. The existence of souvenirs is, therefore, not surprising.

96a (*left*) Globular blue vase with a sepia print of 'St Andrew's Church, Hingham'. Mark: 'Made in Germany' printed in black within concentric circles. Height 2·5″ (6·4 cm.)

96b (*centre*) Fluted pink cup and saucer with moulded and gilded applied decoration. The cup has an overglaze print of 'Cattistock Church' within a gilt circle. Unmarked. Height of cup 2·6″ (6·6 cm.) Diam. of saucer 4·8″ (12·2 cm.)

96c (*right*) Green jug with a black overglaze print of 'St Peter's Church, Hurstbourne Tarrant'. Unmarked. Height 4·8″ (12·2 cm.)

The collector may well wonder what market there was in the small towns and villages such as Hingham (Norfolk), Cattistock (Dorset) and Hurstbourne Tarrant (Hampshire) for pictorial souvenirs. The fact is that these were in the nature of fairings, sold in the markets or nearby fairs, though the churches depicted were notable in themselves. Hingham Church is one of the finest in Norfolk; Cattistock Church had a fine carillon with bells cast in Louvain, in the celebrated foundry of Van Arschodt and, of course, the village is well known for the Cattistock Hunt. St Peter's Church, Hurstbourne Tarrant, revealed early wall paintings after restoration in 1853. However, souvenirs bearing the view of Hurstbourne Tarrant Church, and also of the town of Andover, were undoubtedly made to be sold at Weyhill Fair nearby. Weyhill was celebrated for the great fair held in the neighbourhood for six days, commencing on 10th October, for horses and sheep; the fair was visited by persons from all parts of the Kingdom.

The Victoria and Albert Museum exhibits a Bilston patch box inscribed 'A Present from Weyhill', but with no view; clearly a fairing.

97a Octagonal children's plate with 'daisy moulding' and an underglaze black print, tinted overglaze of 'Windsor Castle'. Unmarked (English, probably from north-east England). Diam. 5·9″ (15 cm.)

97b Pot lid (c 1900) with an underglaze coloured print of Windsor Castle. Diam. 5·7″ (14·5 cm.)

Windsor Castle was begun by William the Conqueror and enlarged and rebuilt by successive monarchs. George IV spent nearly a million pounds on the castle.

The other Royal Palaces shown here on souvenir wares were all built during the lifetime of Queen Victoria. Osborne House was built in the Italian style between 1845 and 1848 from designs by the Prince Consort. The lease of Balmoral estate was purchased by Queen Victoria in 1848 and the castle was built of pink granite some years later in the Scots Baronial style, replacing a smaller mansion which previously occupied the site. Sandringham House in Norfolk was built in 1870 in the Elizabethan style.

98a (*left*) Mug (1872–5) with blue and red rim and an overglaze coloured print of 'Osborne, Isle of Wight'. Mark: H. & A. Manufacturers, Sutherland Rd, Longton, in a circle which encloses the Prince of Wales' feathers. Height 3″ (7·6 cm.). (This was the mark of Hammersley and Asbury, a firm which operated the Prince of Wales Pottery, Longton from 1872–5).

98b (*centre*) Heavy plate with pierced rim (for hanging) with an overglaze coloured print of 'Balmoral Castle' within a wide black band. Unmarked (foreign). Diam. 8·9″ (22·6 cm.).

98c (*right*) Green vase with gilding and an overglaze tinted print of 'Sandringham House, West Front'. Unmarked (foreign). Height 4·4″ (11·2 cm.).

99a (*left*) Cup with an underglaze print (coloured overglaze) with a scene entitled 'Welsh Costumes' and 'A Present from Cardiff' in gilt. Unmarked (English). Height 2·5″ (6·3 cm.)

99b (*centre*) Saucer with gilded rim and an underglaze print (coloured overglaze) with a scene entitled 'Welsh Costumes'. Unmarked (English). Diam. 5·5″ (14 cm.)

99c (*right*) Thinly potted porcelain cup with overglaze sepia print, coloured, of a girl at an 'Irish Spinning Wheel'. Mark: Shield with lion erased, the word 'Bavaria' above and 'Schumann' below. Height 2·4″ (6·1 cm.)

To whom were souvenirs sold as 'A Present from Cardiff'? Perhaps to English visitors who came across the Bristol Channel by steamer from Bristol or Weston-super-Mare. They may have been sold at the resort of Barry Island, or perhaps in the Cardiff market.

The cup with the 'Irish Spinning Wheel' is of particular interest since it indicates that the German souvenir trade catered for visitors to Ireland as well as to English towns and resorts. See also Plate No. 152.

100a (*left*) Jug with gilding and a black overglaze print of an indoor scene—'Taking the Oath for the Gammon of Bacon, Dunmow Town Hall, on June 20th, 1751.' Unmarked (English). Height 4" (10·2 cm.)

100b (*right*) Bowl with gilding and a black overglaze print of an outdoor scene of 'The Dunmow Flitch of Bacon Procession, 1751'. Unmarked (English). Height 2·5" (6·3 cm.)

The ancient custom of the 'Dunmow Flitch', originally connected with the tenure of the abbey lands, is supposed to have been instituted by Robert FitzWalter in 1244. It established a right to a flitch of bacon belonging to the prior and canons on the part of any married couple who 'kneeling on two sharp-pointed stones in the churchyard, swore that they had "not repented them, sleeping or waking, of their marriage in a year and a day" '. The first claim was made in 1445 and the sixth in 1751, when the oath appears to have been taken in the Town Hall. After that date the prize was withheld until after 1855; Harrison Ainsworth had campaigned for the event to be revived. For a period in Victorian times a gammon of bacon was awarded by the Dunmow Agricultural Society to any 'labourer and his wife who shall have brought up the greatest number of children and placed them in respectable service without any, or the least, parochial relief'.

101a (*left*) Plate (c 1874–93) with gilded decoration and a rectangular overglaze black print of 'The Hertfordshire Hermit'. Impressed mark: P within a triangle surmounted by 'D', the whole enclosed within a circle. Diam. 6″ (15·2 cm.)

101b (*right*) Saucer with pink rim and an underglaze black print of 'Lady Godiva and Peeping Tom of Coventry'. Unmarked (English). Diam. 6·3″ (16 cm.)

'The Hertfordshire Hermit' was a Mr James Lucas who was descended from a wealthy Irish family. As a boy he lived with his parents in a house at Redcoats Green, Hertford, a strange child, given to fits of solitude. His parents hoped he would follow the medical profession. As a young man, though intellectual, he was eccentric. When his mother died he watched the coffin for thirteen weeks until the law of sepulchre was enforced. From that time he became a hermit. The rooms of the house were closed, the doors barricaded and he lived in sack cloth and ashes in the kitchen, wearing a blanket and sleeping on a heap of cinders. He spent only £300 a year of his inherited fortune, living mainly on milk and bread. When he died in 1874, seventeen cartloads of ashes were taken from the kitchen. The house was demolished in 1893. During these nineteen years people were attracted to look at the house out of curiosity about its history, hence the local souvenir wares.

Lady Godiva is a historical personage of the eleventh century. The legend is that her husband, Earl Leofric, agreed to a request from his wife to relieve the poor of their taxes, but he insisted as a condition that she should ride naked on a white horse through the city streets. He expected her to refuse, but her natural pity led her to accept the challenge. The local people were threatened with death if they came into the streets or looked out. A tailor is said to have bored a hole in a shutter and peeped out, but as he tried to see the lady on her horse, his eyes dropped out of his head. In the souvenir picture he is hardly a 'peeping Tom'; his head and shoulders appear clearly in the window. The legend appears to have originated in the thirteenth century.

6 British Manufacturers of Pictorial Souvenirs

Ceramic manufacture has been centred in a number of places in Britain but Stoke-on-Trent and its five towns, known collectively as the Potteries, is by far the largest and its wares are known as 'Staffordshire'. There have been literally hundreds of individual firms in existence at one time or another but now their place is taken by a few large combines and only a mere handful of privately-owned firms remain. The only memorial these leave us are the pieces which carry their china marks.

Some of these memorials are humble, but the search for English pieces with English scenes on them is all the more rewarding for being so, and it may well be that this is the first time that anyone has deemed it worthwhile to seek for them. Alas, many of the English pieces are lacking the epitaph in the shape of a china mark.

In 1878 Jewitt, in two large volumes, wrote the history of all the firms then known to have existed. To anyone who has read this sad saga it is a story of endeavour ending all too often in failure and bankruptcy, and another hundred years have not altered the trend. The trouble with potting is that it never required great capital expenditure and it seems that there must be in many people an inherent urge to 'pot', just as there is an urge to till the soil or garden. It is interesting to learn there is a saying in the Potteries that to be a good potter you must be a good gardener. Do not be surprised today to find here and there new kilns being set up, many of them producing pleasant little items for the tourist trade and appropriately called craft pottery. In the old days, before anyone had heard of such people as marketing directors, it was new ideas that counted, new designs and decoration and better quality. In this field of souvenir china it was the tourist or visitor to whom the sales effort was directed.

As long ago as the 1780's a glass and china dealer of Great Yarmouth in East Anglia, called William Absolon, started to decorate some of the pieces he acquired with such phrases as 'A Trifle from Yarmouth', and he painted on them local scenes. Unfortunately, when he died in 1815 there was no one to carry on decorating such souvenir wares, examples of which may be seen in the Norwich Museum.

Similarly the Bilston patch box makers who were operating at roughly the same time with their 'Trifles' and 'Presents from', but with a much wider market, failed to keep going and had disappeared from the scene by 1800, because for some reason their articles lost their appeal or became too expensive.

So to Yarmouth and Bilston goes the honour of starting the pictorial souvenir trade using the inscription of a 'Trifle' or 'Present from', until someone turns up with an earlier claimant; if so, it could be a wooden souvenir with a picture on it. At the beginning of the eighteenth century there were firms like those at Worcester and Derby who were producing wares with attractive pictures of places on them, but they were decorative pieces intended for the gift trade of the time and they were expensive.

102a *(left)* Mug with pink lustre and a black underglaze print of 'The Bridge over the Wear at Sunderland'. On the reverse side is a black print of 'The Gauntlet Clipper Ship'. Unmarked (Sunderland). Height 5″ (12·7 cm.)

102b *(right)* Jug (c 1820–26) with an overglaze tinted print of the 'West View of the Cast Iron Bridge over the River Wear at Sunderland. Built by R. Burden Esq., M.P., Span 236 feet. Height 100 feet. Began 24th September 1793 Opened August 1796'. The reverse side shows a 'God Speed the Plough' print heavily enamelled in red, blue and green with the name of the artist—R. Downing R.A. and of the makers—Dixon Austen & Co., Sunderland. Height 7·7″ (19·6 cm.)

It is to the so-called 'Sunderland ware', the pottery of a number of firms on the North-East Coast, that we owe an era of jugs and mugs which can still be found fairly often, but no longer at give-away-prices. The examples seen in the above Plate show the ever popular Wearmouth Bridge at Sunderland. The range of pictures is limited and they have not hitherto been classed as souvenirs. But they certainly were, for many were bought by sailors visiting the ports. Judging by the number still around in this country, they were popular for a long period, certainly from about 1820 to 1870. A full account of these wares is given in J. T. Shaw's *The Potteries of Sunderland and District* (the latest edition was published in 1968).

After the initial use of the words 'Trifle from' or 'Present from', we have only rarely come across their use again by a British manufacturer prior to the end of the nineteenth century, and yet the Continentals used the words when they started exporting in quantity during the last quarter of the century. As suggested earlier, the British manufacturers must have thought it unnecessary to use the caption on a pictorial souvenir.

In the period up till the Great Exhibition of 1851, apart from Sunderland ware, we have so far seen little more that can be classed as souvenirs, although there are one or two manufacturers of Staffordshire Blue who produced pieces such as T. Carey's Cathedral Series (Plate No. 87). The Worcester factories of Chamberlain and Grainger both produced examples prior to 1851, now both rare and expensive, but it may turn out that there was a good deal more pictorial work done than has yet appeared on the market. There is no doubt that the Exhibition itself stimulated production of souvenir articles of all sorts, which may still be picked up, but they are getting scarcer although souvenirs of the Exhibition of 1862 are in rather better supply. From 1862 onwards there is evidence of an increasing range of British manufactured articles featuring the new seaside resorts, spas, cities, etc., mostly in black on white transfer prints and made in pottery as opposed to porcelain. The British made good pottery and this probably explains the number of large mugs with excellent quality prints which the Continentals did not try to imitate in their hard-paste type of porcelain. Unfortunately, few of these mugs have been marked by the manufacturer and cannot, therefore, be identified.

By the 1880's the growth of the market had attracted the first foreign imports of pictorial souvenirs, following the successful introduction of Fairings in the early 1860's which is referred to later in Chapter 7. At first sight it might be assumed that this new range of imports would perhaps inhibit the continued production of British souvenirs, but at present there is no evidence to suggest that their activities declined. The firm of W. H. Goss pioneered an entirely new range of miniature souvenirs during this period with their Coat of Arms series and extremely good quality small pictorial pieces, which in due course attracted the inevitable imitators, both British and foreign. We regard the period from 1880 to 1914 as the heyday of pictorial ware, in which a number of both British and foreign firms were engaged, and the comparison of the pieces in our collection is interesting. Generally speaking, the British pictures are of a better standard than the foreign and the quality of the pieces is higher, but they were probably more expensive. The Germans and Austrians created a new market for themselves with cheap wares and novelties like cruet sets, using new outlets such as the Bazaars which had sprung up to cater for the growing tourist trade, not only to the seaside but also to London and the big cities.

Although the First World War wiped out the German and Austrian trade, the British never re-established the popularity of pictorial souvenirs and one by one various firms dropped out of the trade, beaten perhaps by snapshots and postcards which increased in number with the popularity of photography, and also by the economic circumstances of the time. Nevertheless, the trade has never entirely disappeared and the collector should not disregard modern pieces which will ultimately prove to be interesting relics of a bygone custom.

It should be noted that, after 1842, firms were able to register designs which were protected for three years. There were diamond shaped marks until 1883 and then serial numbers. They can be most useful in dating wares. The *Handbook of British Pottery and Porcelain* gives the necessary information regarding their interpretation.

We give below a list of makers engaged in the souvenir trade with some notes on their wares and the periods when they were active. It is by no means exhaustive; the collector will undoubtedly trace others to add to the list.

Barker Bros. Ltd., Meir Works, Longton, Staffs.
This firm was established in 1876 and its mark, which often includes a fleur-de-lys, has been noted on souvenir wares.
Barkers & Kent Ltd., Foley Pottery, Fenton, Staffs.
This firm was established in 1889 and an example of its work is seen in Plate No. 103.

103 Moulded orange and green gilded plate with a colour print of 'Loch Promenade, Douglas, Isle of Man'. Mark: A globe with wings. The words 'TRADE MARK' above and makers initials 'B. & K. Ltd.' below. (Note the horse tram and the yachts.)

104 Plate (c 1870) with a hand painted view of Loch Leven on porcelain. The picture is framed in gilt and the rim is pale beige and gilt. Impressed mark 'JB' within a bell. Diam. 9·3″ (23·6 cm.)

J. & M. P. Bell & Co., Ltd., Glasgow

This pottery operated from 1824-1928 and although it had a large output of earthenware it was soon noted for the fine quality of its china, and for its tasteful decoration. J. Arnold Fleming, in his Scottish Pottery (1923), tells us that 'this was accomplished by good artists, most of whom were Scotsmen. Landscapes of Scottish principal 'motifs'.' Indeed, but for all the Scottish touch in the scenery, the painting resembles very much the fine hand-painted china made in these same years in Staffordshire .

The example shown (Plate No. 104) has an impressed mark of a bell which was used by this company from about 1850 to 1870. Whether this may be called a true souvenir or not is open to question. It may have belonged to a dessert service, but it is understandable that people should wish to acquire pieces with such Scottish scenes to remind them of memorable occasions. All such pieces have an appeal to Scottish exiles.

Booths Ltd., Church Bank Pottery, Tunstall, Staffs.
Booths Ltd. made earthenware from 1891. A cup, saucer and plate have prints of Hampstead Church. It is possible that this company, which operated until 1948, produced souvenir wares with other London scenes.

T. & J. Carey, Anchor Works, Lane End, Staffs.
This firm, which operated from 1823 to 1842, produced some fine transfer-printed wares, including a good quality stone china which they called 'Saxon Stone China'. An example is shown in Plate 87.

W. T. Copeland & Sons, Ltd., Spode Works, Stoke-on-Trent, Staffs.

105 The plate illustrated here bears a mark which was used by the Copeland factory between 1857 and 1885. The pattern with its view of Goodwood House was stocked by a retailer in Chichester, which is $3\frac{1}{2}$ miles away from Goodwood, and a town in which racegoers to the annual meeting would be likely to stay. A cup and saucer with similar decoration in green and overglaze prints of Arundel Castle and Arundel Castle Dairy House which bears the name of a dealer (J. Broadbridge, Arundel) appears to have been made by the same firm. Arundel is only about 8 miles from Goodwood and might also have catered for racegoers.

Davenports of Longport, Staffs.
This firm was established in 1794 and continued until it closed down in 1887. T. A. Lockett in his *Davenport Pottery & Porcelain 1794–1887* (1972) records that they produced a certain amount of souvenir ware. Plate No. 39 shows a jug with a print of Eastbourne, and Plate No. 106 (below) was almost certainly produced in 1864 to celebrate the tricentenary of Shakespeare's birth.

THE HOUSE in which SHAKSPEARE was born AD 1564

106 Small porcelain plate (c 1864) with gilt rim and overglaze sepia print of 'The House in which Shakespeare was born AD 1564'. Printed mark: Ribbon with 'Davenport' above an anchor—all in underglaze blue. Diam. 4·3″ (10·8 cm.)

Ford & Pointon Ltd., Norfolk Works, Hanley
This firm was established in 1917 and continued until 1936, though it was part of the Cauldon Group from about 1921. From 1920 onwards it used a swan, on which were the initials 'F & P', as a trade mark.

Wallis Gimson & Co., Lane Delph Pottery, Fenton, Staffs.
This factory was in operation from the end of the eighteenth century with various partnerships, and was well known for its ivory and Queen's ware. The firm of Wallis Gimson & Co. operated for a relatively short period from 1884 to 1890 using a printed beehive as a trade mark. Some pieces are unmarked but the octagonal plates with coloured printed scenes are not difficult to recognise. See Plate No. 82.

William Henry Goss Ltd., Falcon Pottery, Stoke, Staffs.
W. H. Goss, who first set up in business on his own account in 1858, was the outstanding producer of souvenirs during the time of maximum foreign competition from 1880–1914. His porcelain was of the highest quality and he pioneered much smaller items than had previously been offered as souvenirs. As a result of his enterprise and ingenuity, the firm prospered. Goss will be remembered for the great range of small model jugs, jars and vases, some of them Roman, copied from specimens in museums, and on these he placed the heraldic device of the locality in which they were sold. He also used views instead of crests on a small part of this output. Although these pictorial wares are not easy to find, we have seen examples from a collection of some two hundred pieces which include some extremely fine coloured examples besides three varieties of transfer prints—red, sepia and black. Like every successful initiator, it was not long before Goss had his

107 Porcelain souvenirs by W. H. Goss with black overglaze prints.
(*left*) Beaker with a view of Plas Newydd, Llangollen.
(*centre*) Jug with view of Magdalen College, Oxford.
(*right*) mug with view of Ilfracombe Harbour.
All marked W. H. Goss with his falcon trade mark. Height of jug
3·2″ (8·1 cm.)

imitators both British and foreign. There were quite a number of them, but after the First World War the ceramic souvenir trade declined and, by the time the Second War was over, the trade in these miniature souvenirs was dead. Today Goss pictorial items are no longer cheap but they are worth collecting.

Hammersley & Co., Alsagan Pottery, Longton, Staffs.

The plate (108) has a mark which was used by Hammersley & Co., from their establishment in 1887 to 1912. Thereafter they used printed marks which included the word 'England'. The view of Loch Achray in S.W. Perthshire was clearly made as a souvenir piece.

108 Porcelain plate with a hand-painted scene of Loch Achray signed W. Hollins enclosed within a gilt frame. Impressed mark H. & Co., surmounted by a crown. Diam. 9·5″ (24·1 cm.)

Hammersley & Asbury, Prince of Wales Pottery, Longton, Staffs.

These works were established by Benjamin Shirley of Bangor on the wedding day of H.R.H. the Prince of Wales—10th March 1863. Hence the adoption of the Prince of Wales feathers as a china mark. From 1872–5 the pottery was operated by Hammersley & Asbury. According to Jewitt in his *Ceramic Art of Great Britain* (1883), their output included wares with 'local views in colour for sale at watering places, principally for the home market'. These porcelain wares bear overglaze tinted prints and carry a mark with the description 'H & A Manufacturers, Sutherland Road, Longton' on a circular ribbon. Within the circle are the Prince of Wales' feathers. An example of their work is seen in the view of Osborne House on the porcelain mug shown in Plate No. 98a.

A. J. Jones & Sons Ltd., Grafton Works, Longton, Staffs.

This firm made souvenir china from 1900, using the words 'Grafton China' as a trade mark. The mark used consisted of the initials A.B.J. within a Staffordshire knot on a shield, the whole surmounted by a rising sun. See Plate No. 32, showing a mug with a print of Bridlington.

James Kent, Old Foley Pottery, Longton

This firm produced souvenir earthenware plates soon after it started in 1897, and happily is one of the few family firms still in existence, although it no longer makes pictorial souvenirs.

109
Moulded earthenware plate (1901–10) with blue edge and sprayed gilding with a dark blue printed view of 'Windsor Castle'. Mark: an underglaze blue print of a shield surmounted by a crown. A band across the shield bears the initials JKL. Diam. 9·3″ (23·6 cm.)

Mintons of Stoke-on-Trent, Staffs.

This firm, established in 1793, has had a long and distinguished record and has produced much pictorial ware which must be attributed to the gift trade. The large plate marketed by the well-known retailers T. Goode & Sons, London, was no doubt in that category, rather than an expensive souvenir.

110 Large handpainted plate of Warwick Castle with footrim pierced
for hanging. Impressed mark MINTON BB (Best Body). Date
cypher for 1880. Also a printed 'Mintons' mark with globe and the
retailer's name—T. Goode & Co., London. Diam. 15·5″ (39·4 cm.)

*Powell & Bishop, Stafford Street Works,
Hanley*

The original business founded at the end
of the eighteenth century was run by a
variety of Partnerships and it is the use
of the caduceus (the wand carried by
Mercury—a winged rod entwined with
two serpents) as a trade mark which has
provided the only identification amongst
the numerous pieces of black and white
Staffordshire transfer souvenir ware—see
Plate No. 111.

111 Porcelain saucer (1876–8) with overglaze black print 'Ross from Oak Mea-
dows'. Mark: Caduceus trade mark.
Diam. 5·5″ (14·0 cm.)

When the firm became Powell Bishop & Stonier (1878–91) it produced a new earthenware body known as 'Oriental Ivory'. The example shown in Plate No. 112 is a composite souvenir of London.

112 Hors d'oeuvre dish (1882–5) with gilded handle and rim. It has three divisions, each with a tinted print of a London scene—'Royal Exchange', 'The Horse-guards' and 'Albert Memorial'. Mark: A banner with the word LONDON and PBS. A registration mark for 1882: A Chinese man seated on the ground holding an open parasol on which are the words 'Oriental Ivory'. Overall diam. 10·8″ (27·4 cm.)

Ridgways, Bedford Works, Shelton, Hanley, Staffs.
This printed mark was the first to be registered in 1880, although it has 'England' included in it instead of Stoke-on-Trent, and in 1912 there was another mark. This mark appears to have been used in 1912 when it had 'Royal Semi Porcelain' added. The plate is interesting because the picture is a photographic transfer which has not been seen elsewhere.

113 Brown Ridgway plate, footrim pierced for hanging, with a photographic reproduction of the 'Priory Church and Norman House, Christchurch'. Mark: 'Ridgeway' printed across a quiver of arrows. Diam. 9·1″ (23·1 cm.)

Royal Doulton

The jug (*right*) which appears to have an unrecorded mark, shows 'Old Moreton Hall', usually known as 'Little Moreton Hall', a fine Elizabethan timbered building in Cheshire which was inherited by Bishop Abraham in 1912. After expending much devoted care on the building, he offered it to the National Trust in 1937 when a public appeal was made to raise funds to complete the restoration. The current National Trust Guide Book makes no mention of the visit of Queen Elizabeth in 1589, pictured on the jug.

114a (*left*) Pale green vase with tinted print of a golf scene by C. D. Gibson. Mark: 'Royal Doulton, England', surmounted by a crown and lion. Height 3·6" (9·1 cm.)

114b (*right*) Oval earthenware jug with black underglaze print of the interior of 'Old Moreton Hall', with figures in Elizabethan costume (tinted). Inside the rim are the words 'Old Moreton Hall. Visit of Elizabeth 1589'. Mark: Circular underglaze printed circle with 'Old Moreton 1589' in a shield. Above— ROYAL DOULTON. Below—ENGLAND, Height 5" (12·7 cm.)

The unusually shaped vase has a signed cartoon on each side by C. Dana Gibson (1867–1944), the American artist who immortalised the 'Gibson Girls'. The sketch we see is entitled 'Is a caddie always necessary?'; the reverse is 'From 10 a.m. to 6.45 p.m. this dog has been kept out. Where is the S.P.C.A.?' Golfers will note that the clubs are being carried upside down in the golf bag, which was at one time customary. The S.P.C.A. later became the R.S.P.C.A.

John Tams, Crown Works, Stafford Street, Longton.
This firm, which was established c 1875, specialised in toilet wares and government-stamped earthenware measures. See Plate No. 81.

Wildblood Heath & Sons, Peel Works, Longton, Staffs.
This firm operated from 1899 to 1927. After about 1908, they referred to their wares as 'Clifton China'. The initials of the firm, W. H. & S., were given in the mark with 'L' for Longton and, after about 1915, 'Ltd' replaced the 'L'. Wildblood Heath made miniature souvenirs.

Wileman & Co., Foley Potteries and Foley China Works, Fenton, Longton, Staffs.
Wares bearing the initials W. & C. with the word 'England' can safely be attributed to this firm, which operated from 1892 to 1925, often using the words 'Foley China'. However, one should beware of the word 'Foley'. This name was used by a number of Staffordshire potters and was

115 Worcester 'biscuit' vases with views of Low Wood Hotel, Windermere (1907 and Ann Hathaway's Cottage (1906); Trinity House,
Worcester (1907). Mark: Royal Worcester, England, around a circle
surmounted by a crown. Each vase bears a shape number; the
straight sided vases 689, the bulbous vase 161.

derived from the name of a family which owned a good deal of property in Longton. After about
1911, the word 'Shelley' appears in the Wileman mark and, when the Wileman firm ended, the
works became The Shelley Potteries.

Worcester Porcelains

The main porcelain factory at Worcester, founded by Dr Wall c 1751, has had a continuous
history since that date. In 1852 it incorporated the Chamberlain firm and in 1889 the Grainger
firm, which was operated until 1902. During this long period any number of beautiful pictorial
pieces have been aimed at the gift trade market. As has been indicated, the 'gift' was the rich
cousin of the 'souvenir'. Both relied, nevertheless, on tourists and visitors if they were sold at a
spa or other tourist centre; the difference was a matter of price.

The two mugs with feathered handles (Plate No. 10) and prints of Leamington and Great
Malvern are unmarked but can be identified at the Dyson Perrins Museum, Worcester, as the
design used by Mr Binns (of Kerr and Binns, the controlling partnership between 1852 and 1862)
for presents to his God-children.

The Royal Worcester Porcelain Factory Ltd. was formed in 1862 and the marks since that time
have included symbols which make it possible to date marked pieces. The vase showing the Low
Wood Hotel, Windermere, is interesting as a combination of advertising and the souvenir trade.
The Hotel is still operating.

Trinity House, Worcester, was once a hostel of the Grey Friars but was converted to become
the Church House for the diocese.

7 Foreign Manufacturers of Pictorial Souvenirs

As European porcelain was first developed at Meissen in Germany in the early part of the eighteenth century, it really is not surprising that the Germans had a large china industry in the latter half of the nineteenth century and that they also had, like the British, an export trade. The industry on the Continent had been largely built on State Crown patronage and in the case of Germany there were a number of such States extending this patronage before the creation of the German Empire and the unification of 1870. Alongside was the Austro-Hungarian Empire, also represented in our story of pictorial souvenirs, and we shall see how, after 1918, 'Made in Bohemia' turned eventually into 'Made in Czechoslovakia', with the creation of a new State whose wares were still acceptable in England in spite of the War. So when the term 'Foreign' is used in this book it means Germany and Austria, because so far no pictorial souvenir wares have been noted which can be attributed to other European countries prior to 1914.

In the middle of the last century technical developments on the Continent gave them the opportunity of producing new lines for export. These developments included the use of bright colours, particularly various shades of pink, and also of gilding, often generously applied. Added to these advances was the ability to produce cheaply because of low wages. On 1st February 1887, the *Pottery Gazette* was stating that German wages were 40% lower than in Britain and that their operatives were working twelve to sixteen hours a day. By 1st December of that year the Editorial Notes complained that German competition was severe in every direction and that crockery was being imported into England at a lower price than similar English goods could be produced.

The first foreign novelties which were to appear in England were what have now become known as 'Fairings', small china figure groups with English captions depicting English humorous themes and with English sentiment and dress, the earliest dated around 1860. These are fully illustrated in *Victorian China Fairings* by W. S. Bristowe (1971). Like W. H. Goss in England they, in due course, had their imitators and by the 1880's others on the Continent were producing not only the figure groups but decorative wares such as that in Plate No. 116 entitled 'A Present from Southend-on-Sea'. The name 'Fairing' was adopted because their original market in England was the country fair. They also entered the souvenir trade that was rapidly growing at the seaside resorts, in big cities and other tourist centres. There must have been close liaison between the German fairings manufacturers and the people in England who supplied them with the 'script' for the various themes, together with the appropriate costumes. What fun the creators must have had when they started the series! They were, in fact, something like primitive Walt Disneys and, by the price now being paid for them, perhaps belated recognition is being given to their genius.

That these essentially English pieces could be produced on the Continent does indicate that the subsequent production of souvenirs with English views was merely an extension of the liaison already established for the creation of Fairings. The Fairings market certainly preceded imported

116 Fairing with the unusual title 'A Present from Southend-on-Sea'.
Impressed mark: 'Germany'. Height 4·7" (11·9 cm.)

pictorial souvenirs, but could have influenced the development of china novelty souvenirs, of which plenty did not carry a view. It would be interesting to know who revived the idea of using the expression 'A Present from . . .' after so many years. When was it first used by a foreign manufacturer? It was after all appropriate to an article which was purely ornamental, and if there was a view of a named place, it was hardly necessary to add that it was a present from that place. After all, the English hardly bothered to re-introduce the term on their own pictorial souvenir wares.

There was nothing new in the use of views on a new range of china novelties cheaper than anything that had hitherto been made, and the subsequent opening up of a world wide export market. The Scottish woodworking firm, the Smiths of Mauchline, according to the book by E. H. & E. R. Pinto on *Tunbridge and Scottish Souvenir Woodware* (1970), was producing pictorial transfers on wood as early as 1845, and between the years 1860 and 1890 this trade had its maximum prosperity and became world wide. They were certainly exporting to Germany and the Continent, using the appropriate local views. We have in our small wood collection a bodkin case with a view of the Horse Guards Parade and printed underneath the view is 'Made in Germany', so we know that by a date in the 1890's the Germans were exporting woodware to England, probably undercutting Smiths with their lower labour costs. The world-wide trade in Scottish souvenir woodware was emulated by the continental manufacturers, but in china instead of wood. China not only cost less but the pictures were bigger and more easily recognisable than the small views on the wooden pieces. Imitation in those days was the inevitable lot of the successful initiator; the original Fairings were copied and so was Smiths' transfer work. By the last decade of the nineteenth century, cheap china souvenirs had already started the decline in demand for woodware souvenirs. We should also remember that scenic paperweights made of glass, where the picture was stuck on

118

the underside of the glass and magnified, had been developed by the middle of the nineteenth century (see Chapter 9). This trade did not present the same problem as china or wood, however, because the glass shapes could be exported 'in blank' and the pictures stuck on subsequently.

Little is known about the origin of the huge quantity of souvenirs with and without pictures which entered this country between about 1880 and 1914—a period of little more than thirty years. Although this is still within living memory, two World Wars have intervened and effectively swept away people, businesses and national boundaries. Very little information is therefore available.

Taking this country first, the area around Holborn was traditionally the centre of the china trade in London, and before 1914 there were German importing firms based there who must have maintained their own force of travellers. The First World War evoked particularly strong reactions against anything German, and businesses with German sounding names were forced to close down and with them disappeared their records. Perhaps a reader of this book may come across a pattern book which might give us a clue as to the price at which these souvenirs were sold, and how distribution was effected.

Our facts must, therefore, come from over six hundred pieces in our collection, out of which just over one in ten has a china mark whilst a good many more can be attributed to known manufacturers. The following is the list of manufacturers, most of which can be looked up in J. P. Cushion's *Pocket Book of German Ceramic Marks*. See page 122.

Established 1808—P. Donath and its subsidiary Schlesische Porzellanfabrik. Tiefenfurt, Silesia.

       ,,   1898—Greiner and Herda, Oberkotzau, Bavaria.

       ,,   1831—Carl Krister, Waldenburg, Silesia.

       ,,   1900—Max Emanuel & Co., Mitterteich, Bavaria.

       ,,   1755—F. Mehlem, Bonn, Rhineland.

       ,,   1794—Porzellanfabrik Tettau, Tettau, Franconia.

       ,,   1883—Schmidt & Co., Carlsbad, Austria.

       ,,   1871—Carl Schumann, Arzberg, Bavaria.

       ,,   1889—Porzellanfabrik Stadtengsfeld, Thuringia.

       ,,   1811—Unger & Schilde, Roschützer, Porzellanfabrik, Saxony.

It should be noted that five of the above firms were established between 1870 and 1900 and that, of all the factories represented by marks, the only one still in existence, trading under its own name, is Schumann of Arzberg, Bavaria, whose products are today nationally known in West Germany and although we now know its history, following a recent visit (see Chapter 10), we have found no records of their souvenir production or so far of any other manufacturers. The factories situated in Poland, East Germany and Czechoslovakia have all been nationalized, and here there is even less likelihood of any further information being forthcoming. A range of similar souvenirs was sold on the Continent, of which there may be collectors; in the U.S.A., we have ourselves seen a small collection of some forty pieces, all pink, but of an exactly similar range to those sold in Britain; their pictures were particularly interesting. We were able to repatriate one or two English views. There was, therefore, a world-wide trade in pictorial and other souvenirs and there were many more manufacturers than are represented by those who used their china marks; it was a trade using many of the same kind of outlets as the toy market, in which the Germans in particular had a world-wide dominance also, and neither trade ever really recovered from the 1914 War.

The general characteristics of the collection are as follows:

1. Due to the availability of the necessary raw materials practically all the pieces are made of hard paste porcelain, some of it of fine quality, light and very translucent. It seems a pity

117 A collection of pierced plates showing the variety of design,
ranging from 5″ to 9″ in diameter.

a   P DONATH

G.H.O.

BAVARIA

GREINER & HERDA
c

UNGER & SCHILDE
d

b

DONATH SUBSIDIARY
WITH MARK OF ORIGIN

e   TYPICAL MARK
OF ORIGIN

f   TETTAU

MADE IN GERMANY

MAX EMANUEL
g

CARL SCHUMANN
h

i

j
SCHMIDT & Co

k

A U S T R I A
SCHMIDT & Co

l

m   CARL KRISTER

n   UNATTRIBUTED

o   STADTLENGSFELD

FRANZ A MEHLEM
p

122

that some of the transfer prints do not match up to the quality of the china.

2. There is widespread use of pink as a basic background colour, sometimes splashed on rather crudely by hand. But as we shall explain shortly, as so many of the pieces have a mark of origin on them we are of the opinion that the use of pink only became general during the 1890's. It is noticeable that Donath, Schumann and Schmidt of Austria, with the odd exception, did not use pink for their marked pieces. See illustration on the dust jacket.

The range of articles was wide and included those which were useful, such as plates, cups and saucers, teapots, sugar basins and milk jugs, and, although these do not look as though they had ever been used, that may be the reason why they have survived. It is plates, however, which far outnumber any other item in the range and they were intended as ornaments. What is most striking is that three-quarters of them are of the lattice type or have various moulded designs with pierced holes through the body of the plate, some suitable for the insertion of ribbons—hence the expression 'ribbon plates'. Nearly all the identified manufacturers produced plates of this type but Schumann of Bavaria specialised in them and, although not many are marked, their design and style of print is easy to recognise. These plates have already attracted the attention of collectors and, carrying as they do the largest views, they should always prove interesting. We have not yet recorded an English plate of the lattice type belonging to this period.

It would be interesting to know how the orders for foreign pictorial souvenirs were collected in Britain and, more particularly, how the pictures were obtained to make the transfer print; so far we have found out little. The Pintos, however, have been able to tell us how the business of selling woodwork pictorial souvenirs was organised in Britain. They illustrate a pattern book showing the range of objects and the choice of views available for a particular locality, and this must have been taken round by the traveller who worked that area. We can assume that an importing agency, which may well have also been foreign-owned, similarly equipped itself with a sales force of travellers; judging by the out-of-the-way places represented by souvenirs the overall coverage of the country must have been thorough.

Once photography was commercially established, including picture postcards as they were by this period, the building up to an album of views of a locality would not have been difficult, nor transmission to a Continental factory, where the transfer prints were prepared. It must be remembered that this was a seasonal trade with orders being given in the winter months for delivery the following summer holiday season. There was, therefore, an ample time lag even for places as far away as the U.S.A. We believe the transfers to have been made and applied abroad; the evidence to support this view is the odd misspelling of a word and in one case the appearance of the German 'umlaut' over the 'Y' in 'Ryde, Isle of Wight'. What we would like to know is how the transfers were made and in many cases colour-tinted; some again have been made with what appears to be a photographic process, also colour-tinted.

For establishing dates we are helped by an Act of Parliament, Merchandise Marks Act of 1887. Section 2 of the Act states:

Offences as to Trade Marks and trade descriptions—Every person who (Section d.) applies any false description to goods.

Sub-Section 18—after providing for certain exceptions—expressly excludes them. 'Where such trade description includes the name of a place or a country this section shall not apply unless there is added to the trade description, immediately before the name of that place or country in an equally conspicuous manner, with that name, the name of the place or country in which the goods were actually made or produced, with a statement that they were made or produced there.'

This is the explanation for the appearance on so many pieces of the printed circular marks 'Made in Germany', 'Made in Bohemia', 'Made in Austria' etc., but there are also such printed marks as 'Foreign', 'Foreign Manufactured', which would not appear to comply with the Act. What is clear is that to sell 'A Present from Brighton' which was not, in fact, a present from Brighton but made abroad, was a false description and, therefore, an offence under the new Act. We find the following comment in the *Pottery Gazette* of 1st September 1889: 'The law respecting Trade Marks now in force in England, which is far more rigorous than the previous legislation on this subject, has caused considerable dissatisfaction in German industrial circles, its provisions being considered so stringent as to render the import of German articles into England very difficult. The law itself, according to German judgment, is not so objectionable as the severity with which it is applied.' As there were no customs' duties at the time, one cannot imagine a vigorous watch being kept on the proper marking of these imports, and the more likely source of enforcement would be complaints and information laid by someone in the trade against an offending supplier of unmarked goods. The reference to the stringent application of the law may well mean that exporters who merely marked their goods 'Foreign' found out that this was not good enough and subsequently had to comply by stating the country of origin. The pressure must have been such that, with both Britain and the U.S. requiring it, some firms which used china marks thought it less bother to include the country of origin in their china mark.

We therefore find Schumann of Bavaria, Victoria Austria (trading as Schmidt & Co.) and the three stacked rifles of Max Emanuel & Co., with Germany underneath complying in this way whilst the Donath subsidiary which used the crossed swords mark had to stamp their ware 'Made in Germany'.

118 Shaving mug with black overglaze print of the 'High Street and Town Hall, Maidstone'. Impressed 'fish hook' mark (foreign). Height 3·7″ (9·4 cm.)

It can be accepted that anything with a stamp on it denoting foreign origin cannot be of a date earlier than 1888, the year after the Act came into force. It would be convenient to assume that anything without a mark of origin on it should be prior to this date, but some goods obviously slipped through, and Plate No. 118 illustrates this. The left hand car in the print has been identified as a 3 h.p. Benz of 1898 vintage and it has been compared with an actual model which can be seen at the National Motor Museum of Beaulieu, Hampshire. The shaving mug carries no mark except what looks like an impressed fish hook (already noted on other foreign made ware), and as the cars could not have been in existence prior to 1888 this piece, entitled 'High Street and Town Hall, Maidstone', must have been imported immediately before or after 1900. There are other pieces which must have been difficult to stamp, such as egg cups and plant holders, and other unmarked ware can only be studied to see if the date of construction of a building or a pier may be significant.

It must be remembered that the United States' McKinley Tariff Act of 1891 not only imposed a tariff on imports but also required the country of origin to be marked on china imports. The British Merchandise Marks Act of 1887 was aimed at 'false description', there being no custom duty payable; the Americans in their Act of 1891 were beginning their protectionist policy by imposing custom duties: both Acts had the same effect in requiring importers to mark their goods

119 Collection of wares by P. Donath of Tiefenfurt (Silesia).

120 Collection of wares by P. Donath of Tiefenfurt (Silesia).

with the country of origin. It is because the Continentals decided they might as well mark every-thing with their country of origin that most British firms involved in export did the same, adding the word 'England' to their china mark.

Let us now look at what we know about the foreign manufacturers.

P. Donath, Tiefenfurt (Silesia)

Mk. (a). Established in 1808 as hard paste porcelain manufacturers. Tiefenfurt was incorporated into the Polish State with the rest of Silesia after the Treaty of Versailles in 1920, the porcelain industry being nationalised after the last War. In a 1907 Trade Directory, it is listed as producing Table Ware and exporting to France, Britain and America. Its souvenirs covered a wide range in an excellent white porcelain body, and its transfer prints were also good, being applied over the glaze and subsequently tinted by hand—some appear to be based on photographs. The Gothic type captions they used are easy to recognise and the majority of their pieces are marked with a blue crown above a capital S, but not a single piece with this mark carries a stamp of origin.

Schlesische Porzellanfabrik, Tiefenfurt

Mk. (b). Established in 1883 as a subsidiary of P. Donath and reported as having ceased trading at a date unknown. This mark does not appear in J. P. Cushion's book of German Ceramic Marks. Their wares, as can be seen in Plate No. 121, are precisely similar in every characteristic to those of the parent Company shown in Plates Nos. 119 and 120. They have, however, not only different china marks with the crossed swords taking the place of the crown, but also virtu-ally all their pieces are marked with the country of origin, the 'Made in Germany' being in one of two forms. There are one or two pink items of each Donath mark but the pieces with the crossed swords mark are much less numerous than the crown and S, which date as being made prior to 1888. When the British Merchandise Marks Act came in, Donath's must have decided to market their souvenirs through a subsidiary, using a different china mark and complying with the obligation to print the country of origin on their wares. There can have been only one explanation for this move and that was the protection of their higher class, regular business which they did not want associated with the souvenir trade once it became necessary to disclose the country of origin. P. Donath's souvenir wares were probably some of the earliest to be imported into Britain, and they are of higher quality than any subsequent foreign competitors; after they changed the mark in 1888, they ran into a period in the 1890's when competition increased and the general quality of souvenirs deteriorated with the flood of pink ware. Unless they subsequently lowered their standards and produced a new range which we have failed to identify, it looks as though they decided to withdraw from the market and concentrate on their table ware and other better class production. No other explanation can account for the comparative scarcity of pieces bearing the later crossed swords mark, which in any case were probably attributable to the 1890's. It would be interesting to know if a marked item of table ware should ever turn up, but in the meantime a collection of pieces by this manufacturer is well worth having and also ranks as the best in quality by a foreign manufacturer.

121 Collection of wares by Schlesische Porzellanfabrik, Tiefenfurt, the Donath subsidiary.

122 Collection of lustred wares by Greiner and Herda of Oberkotzau (Bavaria).

Greiner and Herda, Oberkotzau (Bavaria)

Mk. (c). This factory uses the capital letters G.H.O. It was established in 1898 and closed in 1943. A marked specimen is a cruet set with a pearl lustre glaze. Pieces with this type of decoration turn up from time to time, and they may well be attributable to this maker.

123 Group of pink wares with sepia prints made by Carl Krister of Waldenburg (Silesia).

Carl Krister, Waldenburg (Silesia)

Mk. (m). Established in 1831 as a general manufacturer of pottery but used the K.P.M. mark. In a 1928 book of ceramic marks it is listed as having been taken over by the well known firm of Rosenthal but the book gives no idea of the date when this took place and, in any case, the factory was situated in Silesia and would have been taken over by the Polish State after the last War. It is interesting that it should at one time have made pottery as the examples we have are good quality porcelain, all in the characteristic pink and their transfer prints executed in a red-brown colour with details clearly shown.

Max Emanuel & Co., Mitterteich (Bavaria)

Mk. (g). This firm was established some time after 1900 as makers of hard paste porcelain and decorators, but is no longer trading under this name, although we know it was taken over by another company. The three stacked rifles mark is in all cases accompanied by a mark of origin and their output appears to have been coloured pink with tinted transfers. Much is unmarked. Their wares appear to be typical of so much of the pink ware that was produced in this period, the only difference being that we know who made it. The quality varies; some of it is crude, some quite respectable, but it was probably cheap. This type of pink ware may well have captured some of the market previously served with slightly better class products.

124 Collection of pink wares by Max Emanuel & Co. of Mitterteich (Bavaria).

Franz A. Mehlem, Bonn (Rhineland)

Mk. (p). This firm was established in 1755 for the manufacture of pottery. A single example has been noted with a circular impressed mark (see Plate No. 81). The mark is difficult to see and collectors are seriously advised to search every piece in their collection in a good light for such evidence of the manufacturer. This piece had been in our collection for a considerable time before we spotted its origin.

Porzellanfabrik Tettau, Tettau, Franconia

Established 1794 as makers of hard paste porcelain. We do not have a pictorial souvenir, only a marked pink fluted saucer.

Carl Schumann, Arzberg (Bavaria)

Mk. (h). This firm was established in 1871 as hard paste manufacturers and decorators and still operates in West Germany, trading under its original name. It is nationally known. It appears from the start to have been the most prolific manufacturer of plates of various sizes, all of the ribbon or lattice type, and their range, as can be seen, extends downwards to small plates, ash-trays and vases. They used a good quality white porcelain, and gilding in one form or another appears on every piece. Not many specimens are marked but the style is so different from that of other factories that it is easy to attribute those unmarked pieces. We believe that the earliest have small black and white transfer views and the majority of the pictures, which cover the whole of the centre area of the plate, are somewhat crudely tinted. There is no single identifiable item using a pink background. It will be noted that the china mark includes the word 'Bavaria'. This served as a country-of-origin mark and no further mark was needed. Pieces without the factory mark sometimes carry the word 'Foreign' or 'Germany' in green; some bear a circular orange 'Made in Germany'.

125 Collection of wares by Carl Schumann, of Arzberg (Bavaria).

126 Pierced plates by Stadtlengsfeld A. G. Porzellanfabrik.

127 A collection of wares by Schmidt & Co., of Carlsbad, Bohemia.

Stadtlengsfeld A. G. Porzellanfabrik, Stadtlengsfeld

Mk. (o). This firm was established in 1889 and were makers of hard paste porcelain. Collectors may find plates by this maker with good quality prints of London in the 1890's. The two examples in our collection show London Bridge and the Royal Exchange in rectangular frames on a pink ground. The moulding is picked out with gilt applied by hand.

Viktoria, Carlsbad (Bohemia)

Mk. (j, k and l). This factory of Schmidt & Co. was established in 1883. Its mark incorporates the word 'Victoria' (English spelling) and 'Austria'. Some unmarked plates with black and white transfer prints have been identified as the work of this firm and, as in the case of Schumann, these are probably pre-1888. They made good class white porcelain but there is no trace that they made any of the pink ware. That they continued in business after the First World War, exporting to Britain, is confirmed by a few items with 'Czechoslovakia' instead of 'Austria' incorporated in the mark (i). The newly-created state of Czechoslovakia was acceptable in England even though Austria was on the wrong side of the War. The views are clearly shown, and gilding is used in many items.

Mk. (i). The Schmidt factory also ran a range of small items under the trade mark 'Gemma' across a shield which has a crown above it. (See Plates Nos. 149, 150 and 151.)

Unger & Schilde, Roschützer Porzellanfabrik (Saxony)

Mk. (d). This factory was established in 1811. It is now in East Germany. Its souvenir wares are of nice, clear translucent porcelain, using a pale pink and characteristic gold gilding, and there appears to be quite a few marked pieces about with the views attractively presented.

128 Collection of wares (pink with the exception of the plate) by Unger & Schilde, of Saxony.

129 Collection of pink wares with unidentified 'S. & K.' or 'red hand' marks.

Unattributed Wares

Some pink pieces bear a mark with 'S. & K.' within the 'Made in Germany' circular stamp. The jug and basin (Plate No. 129) have this mark. The smaller fluted basin and the teapot, however, have a 'red hand' mark together with the 'Made in Germany' mark.

130 Three unattributed shaving mugs and a large lustre chocolate set.
Height of coffee pot: 10″ (25·4 cm.)

131 A miscellaneous collection of unattributed wares.

Many other unattributed wares bear no maker's mark and a selection of these is shown in Plates Nos. 130 and 131. The large chocolate pot, cream jug and basin bear no relation to any of the other wares we have described. The prints are all of London—Tower Bridge, St Paul's Cathedral, the Mansion House, the Houses of Parliament and the Tower of London. These pieces have a gold finish unlike any other lustred souvenir wares we have noted.

Other interesting shapes by unknown makers include cruets, egg cups, shoes and moulded vases with elaborate handles.

8 China Souvenirs in Miniature

We have grouped the miniature china souvenirs together in this chapter at the end of the book because, when photographed, it is desirable to show them separately if the contrast in size is to be appreciated. The largest piece, for instance, is little more than 3″ high and the smallest is only 1″.

These pieces have always had particular attraction for the collector or, indeed, anyone who has a small china cabinet and limited display space. We have already described the work of the English manufacturer, W. H. Goss, in a previous chapter and it is not difficult to appreciate the fine quality of his work from the pieces illustrated below (Plate No. 132). Examples of the English imitations of his work are shown in Plate No. 141. An outstanding foreign manufacturer appears to have been Schmidt & Co. of Austria, whose work is shown in Plates Nos. 149, 150 and 151, all of which carry their china mark.

132 Porcelain souvenirs by W. H. Goss with sepia overglaze prints.
(*left*) Welsh hat with a view of 'Glyn-y-Weddw, Llanbedrog, Pwllheli'
(*centre*) Beaker with a view of the 'Quay and Bridge, Bewdley'
(*right*) Model of Roman Ewer (in Chichester Museum) with a view of 'Arundel Castle'. Registration Mark for 1903.
All marked: W. H. Goss. Height: Jug 2·7″ (6·8 cm.)

133 A pair of porcelain two-handled mugs with views of Gloucester Cathedral and St David's Cathedral respectively. Unmarked (English). Height of larger mug: 1·6″ (4·1 cm.)

134 Reverse sides of the two-handled mugs shown above with tinted sprigs of flowers.

135a (*left*) Blue porcelain mug with overglaze sepia print of 'The Chapel Liten Ruins, Basingstoke'. Mark: 'Made in Germany' within concentric circles. Height 2·1″ (5·3 cm.) (This was more generally known as the Chapel of the Holy Ghost.)

135b (*right*) Gilded porcelain mug with an overglaze painting of a river scene with a bridge and churches in the background. Unmarked. Height 2·2″ (5·6 cm.) (The scene shows the Severn Bridge at Worcester with the spire of St Andrew's Church on the left and the Cathedral on the right.) Possibly made by Grainger of Worcester. See Plate 136b overleaf.

136a The Chapel Liten Ruins at Basingstoke today.

136*b* St Andrews Church by the Severn, Worcester, today.

137*a* (*above*) Shallow jug with black underglaze print of the 'Lifeboat House and Windmill', Lytham, Lancashire. (The reverse side shows 'The Pier, Lytham'.) Unmarked (English).

137*b* (*below*) Cup with black overglaze print of Hastings (note the sailing boats leaving the harbour), and two small mugs with black overglaze prints of 'The Abbey, Bath' and 'Winchester Cathedral', respectively. All pieces unmarked (foreign).

The tiny mugs, each less than 1″ in height, are of particular interest. They were almost certainly made with children in mind and would be suitable for small girls playing with dolls. These are sometimes referred to as 'dolly pieces'. See Plate No. 123 for another view of Winchester Cathedral, using what appears to be the same print.

138 Three porcelain beakers with overglaze tinted views.
    a (left) 'Watersmeet, Lynmouth' and the printed words 'A Present from Ilfracombe' on the reverse side. 'S' over crossed swords in underglaze blue and 'Made in Germany' printed overglaze in brown. Donath subsidiary.
    b (centre) 'Land's End' with 'A Present from Penzance' on the reverse side. Mark of P. Donath.
    c (right) Green beaker with 'The Pier, Littlehampton'. Mark of P. Donath. Height of beakers: 2·6″ (6·6 cm.)

139 Three porcelain vases (c 1899) with overglaze tinted prints of *(left)* 'Dane John, Canterbury'; *(centre)* 'West Gate, Canterbury'; *(right)* 'Hawarden Castle, the Residence of the late W. E. Gladstone'. Each piece has gilding on rim and handles. All unmarked (foreign). Height of centre vase: 3·2″ (8·1 cm.) (*Cassell's Gazetteer* of 1900 states that 'Dane John is an artificial mound which forms an agreeable promenade'.)

140*a* (*above*) Vase with tinted print of 'Brighton' (Metropole Hotel).
140*b* (*below centre*) Vase with tinted view of the 'Crystal Palace'. (*left and right*) Hanging baskets handpainted with a view of Norwich Cathedral framed in a wreath of pink and gilded flowers. All unmarked. Height of large vase 2·8″ (7·1 cm.) (See page 73 for notes on the Crystal Palace).

141 Porcelain water carriers, with sepia overglaze prints of
   a (*left*) 'Carisbrooke Castle'.
   b (*right*) 'The Old Pier, Weston-super-Mare'. Both unmarked (English). Height 2·3″ (5·8 cm.)
   (These are typical examples of the English imitations of W. H. Goss.)

142 Porcelain coal scuttles
   a (*left*) with overglaze tinted print of the 'Church and Castle, Christchurch'. Mark: 'Made in Germany' within concentric circles.
   b (*right*) with black overglaze print of 'St. Mary's Church, Maldon', the sky tinted in blue and the whole surface of the scuttle in pale pink. Unmarked (foreign). Length of longer scuttle: 2·8″ (7·1 cm.)

143a (*left*) Porcelain ark with an overglaze print of the 'Suspension Bridge, Bristol', Mark: 'British Manufacture' in a rectangle. Height 2·3″ (5·8 cm.)

143b (*right*) Porcelain cottage with an overglaze print of a 'View from East Cliff, Bournemouth'. Mark: 'British Manufacture' in a rectangle. Length 2·7″ (6·8 cm.)

144 Porcelain top hat with a black print of 'Robert Burns' on one side and of 'Burns' Cottage' on the other side. Unmarked (English). Height 1·8″ (4·6 cm.)

145 Miniature porcelain shaving mug with 'A Gift from Wells' and a tinted print of a small finch-like bird. Unmarked (English). Height 2·3″ (5·8 cm.) (Although this mug does not carry a topographical scene it has, nevertheless, an interesting shape and unusual scrolled lettering.)

146 Cup and saucer in green, red and gilt with an overglaze print of 'Tower Bridge, London'. Mark on saucer: 'Victoria Austria' with a crown. Diam. of saucer: 4·4″ (11·2 cm.). Diam. of cup: 3″ (7·6 cm.)

147a (left) Fluted cup with saucer with blue and gold around the cup rim. Overglaze tinted print of 'The Beach, Shanklin'. Unmarked: (foreign). Height of cup: 1·8″ (4·6 cm.)

147b (right) Fluted octagonal blue and white cup and saucer with overglaze tinted print of St Austell, Cornwall. Unmarked (foreign). Height of cup: 1·7″ (4·5 cm.)

148 Cup and saucer in pink and yellow with gilded rims. They carry tinted overglaze prints of 'Laxey Wheel, Isle of Man' and 'The promenade, Douglas'. Unmarked (Foreign). Diam. of saucer: 4·2″ (10·7 cm.) Diam. of cup 1·7″ (4·3 cm.)

149a (*left*) Cheese dish in two shades of green with a tinted overglaze print of 'Abbotsford'. Mark: GEMMA on shield beneath a crown. Length of base: 3″ (7·6 cm.)

149b (*right*) Handled tray in two shades of green and some red, with an overglaze tinted print of 'The Wellington Gardens, Great Yarmouth'. Mark: GEMMA on shield beneath a crown printed overglaze with a gilded butterfly.

150 Miniature wares made by Schmidt & Co., Victoria, Austria. Each piece has gilding and green decoration with a silver rim, with a Birmingham hallmark. The coloured prints include (*left*) The Wellington Gardens, Great Yarmouth. Height 3″ (7·6 cm.); (*centre*) Britannia Pier, Great Yarmouth. Destroyed by fire 1909. Height 1·8″ (4·8 cm.); (*right*) The Wellington Gardens, Great Yarmouth. Marks: GEMMA on a shield surmounted by a crown. These Yarmouth pieces also have an overprinted butterfly mark in gilt.

151 Miniature wares by Schmidt & Co., Victoria, Austria, with coloured prints of
a (*left*) Victoria Pavilion, Colwyn Bay. Height 3·1″ (7·9 cm.)
b (*centre*) Combe Martin Church. Height 1·6″ (4 cm.)
c (*right*) Suspension Bridge, Clifton. Height 2·6″ (6·6 cm.)
Mark: GEMMA on a shield surmounted by a crown.

152 Miniature *jardiniere* with stand and bowl, which fit together, both with the same view of Moore Street, Mountmellick, County Cork, Ireland. Height of Stand: 3·2″ (8·2 cm.). Mark: GEMMA on a shield surmounted by a crown. (Mountmellick was a well known lace-making centre which attracted tourists. In Victorian days this type of bowl usually housed an aspidistra, then a popular house plant.)

153 Orange-lustred porcelain box, with circular tinted print on lid of 'Blackgang Chine, Isle of Wight'. Unmarked (foreign). Width 2·2″ (5·6 cm.)

9 Souvenirs of Glass and Other Materials

Glass was used in a variety of ways for producing pictorial souvenirs, the most popular of which were glass paperweights, on the bottom of which were stuck coloured prints and later photographs, the glass acting as a magnifying glass. G. A. Godden devotes a chapter to 'Glass Paperweights' in his book on *Antique China & Glass under £5* (1966) and he tells us that this clever

154 Glass paperweights with coloured prints showing (*top row*) Osborne House; Windsor Castle; The Court House, Carlisle; Crescent, Buxton; Everfield Place, Hastings. (*centre, left to right*) The Pier, Bournemouth; Salisbury Cathedral; Dunluce, C. Antrim. (*bottom row, left to right*) Esplanade, Lowestoft; Brighton; The Toad Rock, Tunbridge Wells; Grand Parade, Eastbourne; Holyrood Palace. The circular weights have curved surfaces: the others have flat surfaces.

development had been thought of by 1851 and that they were sold at the Great Exhibition in that year, and we ourselves have one showing the Royal Family from the painting by Selous.

By the 1870's, in addition to the original dome-shaped weights, other shapes appeared including cubes with bevelled edges which provided alternate views of the same picture. A feature of nearly all the coloured pieces in our collection is that the views appear to have been produced by artists who always placed a group of figures, the ladies in crinolines, in the forefront of the view whatever the subject of the souvenir. Whether they were all done by the same artist is open to doubt, but the style of presentation enlivens the scene and makes them some of the most attractive souvenirs of their time. Unfortunately there is no trace of the makers; the glass shapes were probably imported and the prints produced and stuck on in this country. The paper backing of the prints is in all cases a dark red-brown colour with a stipple effect finish, and in many cases scratches have torn away part of the view; in the absence of perfect specimens, careful restoration is sometimes possible and worthwhile. A selection of these is shown in Plate No. 154.

Plate No. 155 shows a different type

155 Coloured print of 'The Observatory and Playfairs Monument, Edinburgh', mounted behind glass in a heavy brass frame with green baize backing to form a paperweight. Diam. 3·1″ (7·9 cm.)

The use of thin glass was extended into the realms of needle cases and pin holders, using similar style prints as those for the paper weights and being of the same period. The needlecases had the print set under glass in the lid; the pin holders were circular, trimmed with velvet and the reverse side to the view was a mirror. In the examples shown in Plate 155a, the Llandudno piece has a circular wood stand and the print is mounted behind thin concave glass, the article possibly being intended for cosmetic purposes.

In the 1880's the photograph began to replace the coloured print and Mr Godden is able to give us first-hand evidence of how photographs were collected by agents and sent to Germany for the order to be completed in time for the next summer season. Plate No. 156 shows two metal boxes of white alloy, in the lids of which are photographs mounted behind glass; on the one of

155*a* Needle cases and pin holders. Corfe; Llandudno; Hastings; Osborne; Clifton; Carisbrooke; Carnarvon; St Johns, Cambridge.

Weymouth—for all to see—is 'Made in Germany', indicating that the article was made completely in Germany. This is the only piece we have which has a country of origin mark and suggests that a substantial business was done by importing glass articles in the 'blank' and affixing the photographs as required in this country, thus avoiding the necessity for marking. Mr Godden records that Messrs F. Frith & Co., Ltd., of Reigate, Printers and Publishers, operated in this way. We

156 Decorative metal boxes and photographs mounted in the lids.
  a (*left*) Chagford from Lushford Mill.
  b (*right*) Esplanade and Monument, Weymouth. Height 1·1″ (2·8 cm.)

157a (left) Glass inkwell 'Sands & Cliff Clacton'. Height 1·6″ (4 cm.)
  b (right) Glass paperweight 'High Street, Stockton'. Length 2·4″
    (6·1 cm).

158 Glass paperweight with photograph of 'The Promenade, Skegness'.
    4·2×2·5″ (10·7×6·3 cm.)

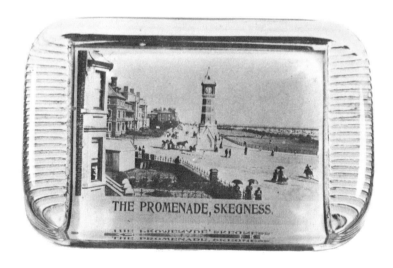

have Plate No. 157, a glass inkwell with a view of Clacton labelled 'Poulton's Artistic Photographs, London, S.E.', and a small rectangular paperweight showing what is obviously an early view of Stockton and marked 'Poulton's Artistic Series', indicating that this firm must have done likewise. What is noticeable is the high quality of some of these tiny prints.

The pieces shown in Plate No. 159 appear to have coloured photographs and have a stronger type of backing. The two taller pieces were priced at 1/6d (7½p).

150

159 Glass paperweights with coloured photographs with views of
    a (*left*) Beachy Head Lighthouse, Eastbourne.
    b (*centre*) Esplanade and Clock Tower, Shanklin. Length 2·9″
        (7·4 cm.)
    c (*right*) Beachy Head, Eastbourne, Height 3·1″ (7·9 cm.)

160*a* (*left*) Glass inkwell with tinted photograph of 'The Needles',
     I.O.W. Height 2·2″ (5·6 cm.)
    b (*right*) Double glass inkwell with photographs of 'Sands from
     Pier E. Bournemouth' and 'Westcliff (Joseph's Steps) Bourne-
     mouth'.

The two photographs of Bournemouth are interesting and probably date around the turn of the century. There is a large crowd on the beach but hardly anyone beyond the edge of the water, and the Westcliff appears undeveloped.

Some photographs were inset in turned alabaster frames supported at the back by a triangular piece of the same material. Alabaster is relatively soft and easy to work. It will take a good polish. We have no evidence as to origin, but the frames could have been imported.

Many articles were made of papier-mâché in Victorian times. Although made of sheets of paper pressed together with flour and glue, this material could be treated like wood when dry. It would seem that a film of photographic material was transferred to the papier-mâché to take the print and that the photograph became an integral part of the tray, rather than a piece of paper stuck onto the surface. Such decoration was sometimes used on pottery (See Wakefield, H. *Victorian Pottery* [1962], p. 36) but such work is rare.

161 Souvenirs of turned alabaster set with glass-covered sepia photographs. (*Top left*) Frame with 'Haddon Hall; (*top right*) Frame with 'Esplanade Pier, Paignton'. J.W. & S.; (*bottom left*) Box with the 'Octagon Church, Wisbech' on lid; (*bottom right*) Frame with 'High Tor, Matlock Bath'. Diam. of largest frame: 3·2″ (7·6 cm.)

162 Papier-mâché tray with photographic view (heavily touched up) of the 'Crystal Palace'. Diam. 3·5″ (8·9 cm.)

163 Rectangular note-jotting case of papier-mâché with handpainted view of 'Keswick' and on the reverse side an unnamed Lakeland scene. The jotting card within is dated May 1st, 1858. Length 3·9″ (9·9 cm.)

Apart from the smaller glass souvenirs already described, larger coloured prints were sometimes mounted behind thin sheets of glass for wall decoration. These were 'framed' by sticking the glazed print to a thin piece of board covered with velvet. A loop was provided so that the picture could be hung on the wall.

Finally, a curious group of glass souvenirs which sometimes have the description 'GENUINE DOLHAIN WIRTHS' printed on the back, were handpainted by a skilful artist on glass shapes in considerable variety (Plates Nos. 166–7).

The glass used was white and was similar to that in everyday use for the manufacture of the common type of white lampshade—now no longer seen.

The palette used was mainly of grey, brown and green and the highlights on trees and vegetation were obtained by using flecks of white. Some are signed W. Wirths. So far, however, it has

164 Glass picture, printed and tinted, mounted on green velvet. St Paul's Cathedral.

165 Glass picture, printed and tinted, mounted on green velvet. Westminster Abbey and St Margaret's Church.
Each picture 7″ (17·8 cm.) square.

been impossible to gather any useful information about the firm that made them or the artist who decorated them. Dolhain is in the east of Belgium. We do not know if the painting was done there or in England. It seems likely that these souvenirs may have been sold by Wirths Brothers & Owen, who had premises at 15 Long Lane, London, from 1884. A factory at Klosterle in Bohemia appears to have copied these souvenirs, producing cheap frosted glass mementoes with hand coloured transfer prints signed P. Jost. This firm ceased to operate c. 1895. Perhaps it was this competition that forced the Wirths firm to name their products 'Genuine'.

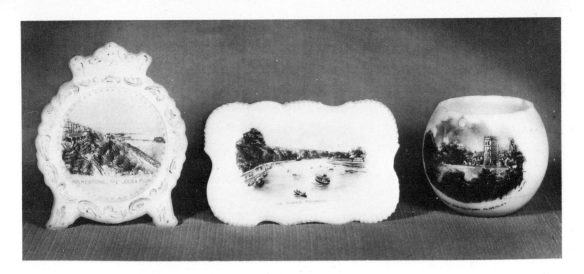

166 White matt-surfaced moulded glass souvenirs with handpainted views by W. Wirths. (*left*) Folkestone, The Lees and Pier; Height 4·4″ (11 cm.) (*centre*) The Thames, Richmond; Length 5″ (12·8 cm.) (*right*) Church and Rectory, Alderley.

167 Opaque white souvenirs with handpainted views by W. Wirths 'On the Canal, Llangollen' and 'Castle Street, Buckingham'. Height 6·5″ (16·3 cm.) Diam. 7″ (17·8 cm.)

168 The Porzellanfabrik Mitterteich in Bavaria which prior to 1917 was operated by the Max Emanuel Company, makers of souvenir wares.

169 The entrance to the Schumann factory at Arzberg in Bavaria. Note the lion mark in the stonework which appears on their nineteenth century souvenir wares.

10 The End of a Story
by A. W. COYSH

To all readers of this book it will now be clear that most of the pictorial souvenirs sold in the seaside resorts and tourist centres of Britain between about 1880 and 1914 were made in Germany or Austria. There were several centres of production including Bavaria, Bohemia, Saxony, Silesia and Thuringia, all within easy reach of china clay and fuel. The story of the firms involved has been pieced together by the author from marked wares in his extensive collection. One point worried him. Might it be possible to find out more about these souvenirs in the places where they were made? He asked me to undertake a journey to Germany to investigate.

The last sixty years have produced great changes in Europe. Two World Wars not only spread destruction; they also changed the map. Saxony, Silesia and Thuringia now lie mainly in East Germany. The china clay areas of the old Austria are now within Czechoslovakia. Unfortunately, the managements of the porcelain factories in these countries, no doubt for good reasons, do not encourage strangers. The main chance of success clearly lay in a visit to some of the factories in Bavaria which lie between the heavily wooded Fichtelgebirge and the Czech border. These are scattered over a wide area in a belt which extends some eighty kilometres from Hof in the north to Weiden in the south, mainly in small towns and villages.

An exploration of this area led to the discovery of two factories which were engaged in the souvenir trade at the turn of the century; others had disappeared or had turned over to the production of electrical insulators. It was known that a firm called Max Emanuel & Co. had operated at Mitterteich. This factory was taken over in 1917 by the present Porzellanfabrik Mitterteich (see Plate No. 168) and no records of the old company were kept. When I showed the works manager a pink plate bearing a printed view of Plymouth (similar to those in Plate 124) I might just as well have been handing him a piece of lunar rock until he turned the plate over to look at the 'back mark', in this case a red-printed mark of three stacked rifles. 'Yes', he said, 'this *must* have been made in this factory; that was the mark of Max Emanuel.' He knew nothing at all, however, about the production or distribution of such souvenir wares.

A visit to Arzberg, a few miles to the north, proved more rewarding for the same firm has operated there since 1871. The factory announces its presence on the facade of a roadside entrance—CARL SCHUMANN (Plate 169). Beside the name is the factory mark, a shield with lion erased, similar to the mark seen on souvenir wares. This firm has always been associated with the Schumann family though it has grown over the years until it now employs well over a thousand workers. After a short conversation with a senior member of the staff who had served the organisation for some forty years, I produced a little cup with the Schumann mark which also bore a coloured view entitled 'Irish Spinning Wheel' (see Plate No. 99c). All he could say was: 'This must have been made years ago when we were importing clay from Sweden. Those supplies are now exhausted and we get much of our clay from Cornwall.' The cup had a technical significance for him but although he knew that the firm had produced souvenir wares, he had no knowledge of the way in which the pictures were obtained or of the method of distribution of the wares themselves. He explained that what records had existed were destroyed when a bomb struck a wing of the factory during the Second World War. Since then it has been the custom in most of the porcelain factories to destroy their records after the statutory period of seven years during which they must be kept. However, after some time a well-worn pattern book was found dating back to 1945. A search revealed that there had been one special order for souvenir ashtrays in 1948 which were printed with the view of a town in Uruguay!

The wares produced by the Schumann factory today, most of which are in the modern style, include some traditional designs. They make beautifully painted dessert services, for example, with pierced dishes and baskets. The factory has, apparently, always prided itself on pierced work and in 1914 a member of the Schumann family produced the first mechanical device for piercing the ceramic body. Before that date the pierced wares were moulded and the holes were then tidied up by hand using a sharp knife. This was the method used to produce the ribbon plates which are so widely collected today.

Before leaving the factory the little souvenir cup was handed over and I was assured that this would 'start our collection'. The story of the vast trade in the pre-1914 souvenir wares has disappeared without trace in West Germany and likewise in East Germany, Poland and Czechoslovakia, where there has been over a quarter of a century of State ownership. It may seem extraordinary that a stranger should introduce them to a business they originally pioneered, but it serves to confirm a fascinating story about pictorial souvenirs, of which there remains ample evidence here but none in the countries of origin.

Glossary

Biscuit: the name given to porcelain or pottery fired in an unglazed state.

Body: the material of the potter's clay, or the ware itself.

Earthenware: another name for pottery.

Glaze: a translucent vitreous coating applied to porcelain and pottery which protects the body and gives the ware a sheen.

Hard-paste: porcelain made from china clay and china stone. It shows a shining surface when fractured.

Lustre decoration: a thin film of metallic colouring on pottery or porcelain.

Moulding: the shaping of the body or decoration of pottery or porcelain in a mould. After about 1750, plaster was used for moulding ceramics.

Overglaze: decoration painted or printed on ceramics after the glaze has been fired.

Paste: the body used for porcelain.

Porcelain: translucent ceramic wares after firing.

Pottery: opaque ceramic wares after firing.

Print: printing on wood, pottery and porcelain was done by transference. An engraving was made on a copper plate and a print was taken on paper. This paper was then transferred to the material to be decorated.

Soft-paste: a porcelain body which can be fired at a lower temperature than hard-paste porcelain.

Underglaze: decoration painted or printed on ceramics before the glaze has been applied and fired. Such decoration is protected by the glaze and does not rub off, as some overglaze decoration is liable to do.

Index

(Page numbers only)